SCOTUS 2020

Morgan Marietta
Editor

SCOTUS 2020

Major Decisions and Developments
of the U.S. Supreme Court

Editor
Morgan Marietta
Department of Political Science
University of Massachusetts Lowell
Lowell, MA, USA

ISBN 978-3-030-53850-7   ISBN 978-3-030-53851-4   (eBook)
https://doi.org/10.1007/978-3-030-53851-4

Cover design by Oscar Spigolon and eStudio Calamar

This Palgrave Macmillan imprint is published by the registered company Springer Nature Switzerland AG
The registered company address is: Gewerbestrasse 11, 6330 Cham, Switzerland

Contents

Notes on Contributors

Lawrence Baum is Professor Emeritus of Political Science at Ohio State University. The primary focus of his research is explanation of judges' choices as decision-makers. His most recent books are *Ideology on the Supreme Court* (Princeton University Press 2017), *The Battle for the Court: Interest Groups, Judicial Elections, and Public Policy* (University of Virginia Press 2017, with co-authors David Klein and Matthew Streb), *The Company They Keep: How Partisan Divisions Came to the Supreme Court* (Oxford University Press 2019, with co-author Neal Devins), and *The Supreme Court*, 13th edition (CQ Press, 2019).

Joseph Bolton is a Ph.D. Candidate and Graduate Instructor at Washington State University. His research focuses on media and the courts, political polarization, and the determinants of counter-partisan behavior.

Jennifer Bowie is Associate Professor of Political Science at the University of Richmond in Richmond, Virginia. She is the Editor of the *Law and Politics Book Review* and is a co-author of *The View from the Bench and Chambers: Examining Judicial Process and Decision Making on the U.S. Courts of Appeals* (University of Virginia Press, 2014 with Donald

R. Songer and John Szmer). Her research has appeared in a number of journals including *The Journal of Politics*, *Political Research Quarterly*, and *The Journal of Law and Courts*, and also has been funded by the National Science Foundation.

Cornell Clayton is Director of the Thomas S. Foley Institute for Public Policy and Public Service at Washington State University, where he is also the C.O. Johnson Distinguished Professor in Political Science. He has published widely on American government, politics, and law, and is the author or editor of 8 books and more than 60 scholarly journal articles and book chapters. His research twice received the American Judicature Award from the American Political Science Association. He previously served as editor of *Political Research Quarterly*.

Paul M. Collins Jr. is Professor of Legal Studies and Political Science at the University of Massachusetts Amherst. His research focuses on understanding the democratic nature of the judiciary, interdisciplinary approaches to legal decision-making, and social movement litigation. The recipient of numerous research awards, he has published three books and more than 30 journal articles. Collins' research and commentary have appeared in a host of popular media outlets, including CNN, the *New York Times*, and the *Washington Post*.

Justin Dyer is Professor of Political Science at the University of Missouri and founding director of the Kinder Institute on Constitutional Democracy, an interdisciplinary center for the study of American political thought and history. He is the author of *C.S. Lewis on Politics and the Natural Law* (Cambridge, 2016, with Micah Watson); *Slavery, Abortion, and the Politics of Constitutional Meaning* (Cambridge, 2013); and *Natural Law and the Antislavery Constitutional Tradition* (Cambridge, 2012), and co-editor of the two-volume constitutional law casebook, *American Constitutional Law* (West Academic Press, 2018).

John C. Eastman is the Henry Salvatori Professor of Law & Community Service, and former Dean, at Chapman University's Fowler School of Law. He holds a J.D. from the University of Chicago, a Ph.D. in Government from Claremont Graduate School, and clerked for Justice Clarence Thomas. For the 2020–2021 academic year, he will be the

Visiting Scholar in Conservative Thought and Policy at the University of Colorado Boulder's Benson Center for the Study of Western Civilization. He is a senior fellow at the Claremont Institute and founding director of the Institute's Center for Constitutional Jurisprudence, on whose behalf he filed an amicus curiae brief in *DHS v. University of California* on the DACA rescission.

Julia Bess Frank is Professor Emeritus of Psychiatry and Behavioral Sciences at George Washington University School of Medicine and Health Sciences. She teaches and practices psychiatry in the Washington, D.C. area, and he conducts forensic mental health evaluations of asylum-seeking individuals for Physicians for Human Rights and the Georgetown University Law School asylum clinic. Dr. Frank is co-editor of *The Behavioral Sciences and Health Care*, 4th edition (2018), as well as co-author of *Persuasion and Healing: A Comparative Study of Psychotherapy*, 3rd edition (1991), among other publications on psychiatric evaluation, women's mental health, psychological trauma, and psychiatry education.

Mark A. Graber is the Regents Professor at the University of Maryland Carey School of Law. He is the author of *A New Introduction to American Constitutionalism*, co-editor (with Keith Whittington and Howard Gillman) of *American Constitutionalism: Structures and Powers* and *American Constitutionalism: Rights and Powers*, and co-editor (with Mark Tushnet and Sanford Levinson) of *Constitutional Democracy in Crisis?* (all from Oxford University Press). He is presently working on *The Forgotten Fourteenth Amendment*, a study of the Fourteenth Amendment Republicans drafted in 1866 rather than the Fourteenth Amendment that is litigated at present.

Rebecca Hamlin is Associate Professor of Legal Studies and Political Science at the University of Massachusetts Amherst. Her research focuses on the politics of asylum, immigration, and refugee law, both in the United States and in comparative perspective. Along with numerous articles, she is the author of *Let Me Be a Refugee* (Oxford University Press, 2014) and the forthcoming *Crossing: How We Label and React to People on the Move* (Stanford University Press, 2021).

Erin Hawley is Senior Fellow at the Kinder Institute and former Associate Professor of Law at the University of Missouri School of Law. She serves as a public member of the Administrative Conference of the United States. Erin's research interests include the separation of powers, federal courts, agricultural law, and administrative law. Her work has been published in numerous top law journals and she is a frequent national commentator on legal issues. She is a former clerk to Chief Justice John G. Roberts Jr. of the Supreme Court of the United States and Judge J. Harvie Wilkinson III of the U.S. Court of Appeals for the Fourth Circuit, and served as Counsel to United States Attorney General Michael Mukasey at the Department of Justice.

David Klein is Professor and Department Head at Eastern Michigan University. He served as the inaugural editor of the *Journal of Law & Courts* (2011–2017) and is the author of three books: *Making Law in the United States Courts of Appeals* (Cambridge University Press, 2002), *American Courts Explained: A Detailed Introduction to the Legal Process Using Real Cases* (West Academic Publishing 2016, with Gregory Mitchell), and *The Battle for the Court: Interest Groups, Judicial Elections, and Public Policy* (University of Virginia Press, 2017, with Lawrence Baum and Matthew Streb).

Morgan Marietta is Associate Professor of Political Science at the University of Massachusetts Lowell. He is the author of four books, *The Politics of Sacred Rhetoric, A Citizen's Guide to American Ideology, A Citizen's Guide to the Constitution and the Supreme Court*, and most recently *One Nation, Two Realities: Dueling Facts in American Democracy* on the causes and consequences of polarized perceptions of facts. His current book project is *The Supreme Court of Facts*, examining the Court's rulings on perceptions of evolving social realities. He is the co-editor of the *Citizen Guides to Politics & Public Affairs* and editor of the annual *SCOTUS* volume.

Natasha Markov-Riss is a recent graduate of Swarthmore College, where she majored in Political Science, double minored in Film and Media Studies and Peace and Conflict Studies, and graduated Phi Beta Kappa. She is currently living on Peaks Island, Maine, where she runs a golf cart rental business for tourists. Natasha is also a part-time researcher for Ethix.AI, an MIT-based think tank tackling issues of algorithmic bias. In January, she will begin her Fulbright on the Canary Islands.

Carol Nackenoff is Richter Professor of Political Science at Swarthmore College, where she teaches constitutional law and American politics. She received her Ph.D. from the University of Chicago. She is the author of *The Fictional Republic: Horatio Alger and American Political Discourse* (1994), co-author (with Julie Novkov) of a forthcoming volume on *Wong Kim Ark* and birthright citizenship in the United States, and she composed the entry on the Supreme Court for Oxford Bibliographies Online. She co-edited *Statebuilding from the Margins* (with Julie Novkov, 2014), *Jane Addams and the Practice of Democracy* (with Marilyn Fischer and Wendy Chmielewski, 2009), and *Stating the Family: New Directions in the Study of American Politics* (with Julie Novkov, 2020). Her current research examines conflicts over the extent and terms of incorporation of women, African Americans, Native Americans, workers, and immigrants into the polity between 1875 and 1925, and the role organized women played in shaping new definitions of public work in American politics.

Julie Novkov is a Collins Fellow and Professor of Political Science and Women's, Gender, and Sexuality Studies, at the University at Albany, SUNY. Her research and teaching address law, history, US political development, and subordinated identity. She is the author of several books and co-edited volumes, including the award-winning *Racial Union*. She chaired the Political Science Department from 2011–2017 and was President of the Western Political Science Association from 2016–2017. She is currently a member of the path-breaking twelve-woman team responsible for editing the *American Political Science Review* from 2020 through 2024.

Kevin Pybas is Associate Professor of Political Science at Missouri State University, where he teaches constitutional law and American politics. His research focuses on the Supreme Court's religion jurisprudence, church–state relations in the founding era, and contemporary liberal political thought. He has published numerous articles and book chapters on these topics.

Gerald N. Rosenberg taught Political Science and Law at the University of Chicago for thirty-five years. Trained as both a Political Scientist and a lawyer, his work focuses on the interaction between courts, social movements, and the society and culture in which they are embedded. He is the author of *The Hollow Hope: Can Courts Bring About Social Change?* (3rd edition forthcoming, 2021), a textbook on American Government, and is co-editor of *A Qualified Hope: The Indian Supreme Court and Progressive Social Change* (2019). His work has appeared in numerous law reviews, journals, and edited collections.

Austin Sarat is Associate Provost, Associate Dean of the Faculty, and William Nelson Cromwell Professor of Jurisprudence & Political Science at Amherst College. He is currently the editor of *Law, Culture and the Humanities* and of *Studies in Law, Politics, and Society*. He is the author or editor of more than 90 books. His publications include *The Death Penalty on the Ballot: American Democracy and the Fate of Capital Punishment* (Cambridge University Press, 2019), *The Lives of Guns* (Oxford University Press, 2018), and *Gruesome Spectacles: Botched Executions and America's Death Penalty* (Stanford University Press, 2014).

Howard Schweber is Professor of Political Science and an affiliate faculty member of the Law School at the University of Wisconsin-Madison. Prof. Schweber received his Ph.D. from Cornell and his JD from the University of Washington. He is the author of four books and co-editor of two others, as well as having written numerous articles on topics relating to constitutional law, democratic theory, and American political development. Prof. Schweber is the editor of *Constitutional Studies*.

1

Introduction: The 2019–2020 Term at the Supreme Court

Morgan Marietta

The 2019–2020 term of the Supreme Court was the most eventful in decades. The significance and sheer number of the major cases was stunning. This year's rulings focused on LGBT discrimination, abortion regulation, subpoenas of the Trump administration, the Electoral College, immigration, Native rights, the rights of noncitizens, the Second Amendment, church and state, presidential power over executive agencies, and criminal justice concerns about unanimous juries, the insanity defense, and public fraud. The range of constitutional and legal controversy is remarkable, raising questions about the nature of representation in our elections, religious liberty, restitution for the violation of constitutional rights, the separation of powers between the Congress and the presidency, the role of precedent as a controlling doctrine of constitutional law, the proper way to read the text of laws, and how the Court comprehends evolving social realities.

M. Marietta (✉)
Department of Political Science,
University of Massachusetts Lowell, Lowell, MA, USA

© The Author(s) 2021
M. Marietta (ed.), *SCOTUS 2020*,
https://doi.org/10.1007/978-3-030-53851-4_1

1

While many of these controversies were being considered, the Chief Justice presided over the impeachment trial of the President in the US Senate (as Article I, Section 3 of the Constitution requires). The proceedings of the Court were also interrupted by the Covid-19 pandemic, leading to the replacement of the traditional oral arguments in front of the Justices by arguments over the telephone under new rules for questioning.[1] The combined delay led to the final rulings being rendered in mid-July, the first time the Court's season went this late in two decades. All of this transpired against the backdrop of the 2020 presidential campaign, with many of the major cases having not only constitutional but also powerful partisan implications.

To summarize the year's major rulings, they

1. Expand the prohibition of employment discrimination "on the basis of sex" under the Civil Rights Act of 1964 to include LGBT employees,
2. Allow states to ban "faithless electors" by requiring presidential electors to abide by their state's popular vote,
3. Overturn the Trump administration's rescission of the Obama administration's DACA program on the grounds that the Administrative Procedure Act (APA) requires a full disclosure and discussion of the relevant facts including the reliance interests of the DACA recipients who would be affected,
4. Overturn state limitations on the participation of religious schools in public benefit programs; uphold exemptions for religious organizations with objections to the Obamacare contraception mandate; and affirm the autonomy of religious schools to select teachers under the "ministerial exception" to employment regulations,
5. Disallow noncitizens from bringing suits for damages in federal courts as a remedy for excessive force by US agents when the event occurred beyond US borders,

---

[1]See TheConversation.com, "Supreme Court Phoning It in Means Better Arguments, more Public Engagement" (9 June 2020).

6. Overturn Louisiana's abortion regulations requiring practitioners to hold admitting privileges at a local hospital, upholding the precedent from *Whole Woman's Health* in 2016,

7. Allow individual states to limit the boundaries of the insanity defense grounded in competing perceptions of mental illness,

8. Limit convictions for fraud under federal law to demonstrable cases of self-enrichment, but not diversion of funds for political purposes as in the Bridgegate controversy,

9. Recognize that the Creek Indian reservation in Eastern Oklahoma—established by treaties in the 1800s—has never been disestablished by Congress, meaning that tribal sovereignty continues within Creek Nation boundaries and that major crimes must be tried in federal rather than state court,

10. Dismiss a claim of a constitutional violation when the local government has withdrawn the disputed regulation (making the original claim moot, in this case regarding gun regulation under the Second Amendment),

11. Disallow nonunanimous juries for criminal convictions under the Sixth Amendment,

12. Strike down the congressional limitation of the President to remove the head of a federal agency such as the Consumer Finance Protection Bureau as a violation of the separation of powers between the executive and legislative branches of the federal government,

13. Allow the President to resist congressional subpoenas that do not have a clear connection to ongoing legislation, and reject the claim of absolute immunity of the President from subpoenas from local prosecutors investigating a possible criminal charge.

Table 1.1 2019–2020 major cases[a]

Ch.	Case	Issue	Vote	Majority & Author
2	*Bostock*	LGBT discrimination (statutory interpretation of Title VII)	6-3	4 liberals +Gorsuch, Roberts (Gorsuch)
3	*Chiafalo*	The Electoral College (federalism)	9-0	unanimous (Kagan)
4	*DHS v. U. of Cal.*	Executive power (statutory interpretation, reliance interests)	5-4	4 liberals +Roberts (Roberts)
5	*Espinoza*	Religious liberty (Free Exercise v. Establishment)	5-4	5 conservatives (Roberts)
	Lady of Guadalupe	Religious liberty (Free Exercise v. employment regulation)	7-2	5 conservatives +Breyer, Kagan (Alito)
	Little Sisters of the Poor	Religious liberty (statutory interpretation of ACA, APA, RFRA)	7-2	5 conservatives +Breyer, Kagan (Thomas)
6	*Hernández*	Noncitizen rights (restitution for constitutional violations)	5-4	5 conservatives (Alito)
7	*June Medical*	Abortion regulation (precedent, federalism)	5-4	4 liberals +Roberts (Breyer)
8	*Kahler*	Insanity defense (social facts, federalism)	6-3	5 conservatives +Kagan (Kagan)

Table 1.1

Ch.	Case	Issue	Vote	Majority & Author
9	*Kelly*	Public fraud (statutory interpretation)	9-0	Unanimous (Kagan)
10	*McGirt*	Native rights (statutory interpretation)	5-4	4 liberals +Gorsuch (Gorsuch)
11	*NY Rifle & Pistol*	2nd Amendment (mootness)	6-3	4 liberals +Kavanaugh, Roberts (unsigned)
12	*Ramos*	Nonunanimous juries (precedent)	6-3	3 conservatives +3 liberals (Gorsuch)
13	*Seila Law*	Presidential power (separation of powers)	5-4	5 conservatives (Roberts)
14	*Trump v. Mazars*	Presidential power re: Congress (separation of powers)	7-2	4 liberals +3 conservatives (Roberts) (Alito, Thomas dissent to the right)
	Trump v. Vance	Presidential power re: state prosecutors (separation of powers)	7-2	4 liberals +Gorsuch, Kavanaugh, Roberts (Roberts)

[a]*Issue* describes the broad topic at hand (with major areas of constitutional or legal doctrine in parentheses). *Vote* describes the majority and dissenting positions among the nine Justices. *Majority & Author* notes the general ideological grouping among the Justices (with the author of the majority opinion in parentheses). In general, the five conservative Justices are considered to be Chief Justice Roberts (appointed by George W. Bush), Samuel Alito (George W. Bush), Neil Gorsuch (Trump), Brett Kavanaugh (Trump), and Clarence Thomas (George H. W. Bush); the liberal Justices are Stephen Breyer (Clinton), Ruth Bader Ginsburg (Clinton), Elena Kagan (Obama), and Sonia Sotomayor (Obama)

Statutory Interpretation (LGBT Rights, Native Rights, Public Fraud, Immigration)

One of my favorite definitions of constitutional democracy is "self rule under law."[2] The words carved into the Supreme Court building express a commitment to "equal justice under law." In either formulation it is the Court's role to interpret and explain the words on paper that bind unruly humans to a democratic outcome. Those laws include both our *basic law* (the Constitution) and our *statutory laws* (passed by the national and state legislatures). Some of the Court's most politically divisive rulings have dealt with statutory law, including the rulings on Obamacare in 2015 (*King v. Burwell* over the meaning of the Affordable Care Act) or on voting rights in 2018 (*Husted* over the meaning of the Motor Voter Act), among many others. This year several of the major cases dealt with influential disputes over the specific meaning of congressional laws, including the controversies over *LGBT rights, Native rights, public fraud*, and *immigration.*

LGBT rights. One of the landmark cases in a crowded year was the decision on gay rights in *Bostock v. Clayton County.* In Chapter 2, Julie Novkov discusses the three cases consolidated in this controversy: Gerald Bostock was fired by Clayton County, Georgia, because he is gay; Donald Zarda was fired from his job as a tandem skydive instructor for being gay; and Aimee Stephens transitioned from male to female identity and was fired from her job as a funeral director. Whether each of these actions violates the law reduces to a question of statutory interpretation: what does the word "sex" mean in Title VII of the Civil Rights Act of 1964? The language of the Constitution is not at issue, but instead the language of one of the most influential laws of the twentieth century. The phrase "because of sex" clearly protects women who are not hired, not promoted, or fired because of their gender, but what about gay or transgender employees? In a 6-3 decision written by conservative Justice Neil Gorsuch and joined by Chief Justice John Roberts, the Court ruled

---

[2]See Christopher Harmon, *A Citizen's Guide to Terrorism and Counterterrorism* Chapter 3, 2nd Ed. (Routledge, 2020).

that the existing language from 1964 also protects LGBT employees, a milestone in the history of gay rights.

Statutory language like "because of sex" could mean different things if we follow different theories of interpretation. Some argue that we should focus on the *purpose* of a statute; others reject this approach in favor of a strict reliance on the *text* itself. The first group argues that written law is often inexplicable without reference to its purpose; the second group argues that judges will inevitably substitute their own preferences when attempting to discern intent, robbing citizens of representation and circumventing legislatures by "fixing" their laws for them without accountability to constituents.[3]

The balance between broad purpose and specific text might be solved by employing the *canons* of statutory interpretation, or the recognized rules that have evolved over centuries of legal practice. Even this approach, however, has limitations for a simple reason: "there are two opposing canons on almost every point," as the famed legal scholar Karl Llewellyn pointed out in 1950.[4] As Llewellyn phrased it, for almost every "thrust" there is a "parry." Some of the inherent contradiction results from the long-standing debate between purpose and text. On the one hand, laws are intended to solve problems and guide conduct; they are not mere rules without point. On the other hand, written laws must be clear and binding in order to function, so they must convey distinct limits rather than vague concepts that no two people will understand the same way. Law has both broad purpose and explicit boundaries. The question is often which of the two concepts takes the lead.

The term for focusing on the specific language rather than the broader purpose is *textualism*, an approach famously championed by Justice Antonin Scalia (on the Court from 1986 to 2016).[5] Justice Neil Gorsuch (Scalia's replacement in 2017) claims a strong adherence to this approach,

---

[3]See Robert Katzmann's, *Judging Statutes* (2016), as opposed to Antonin Scalia's, *A Matter of Interpretation* (1997).

[4]Karl Llewellyn, "Remarks on the Theory of Appellate Decisions and the Rules or Canons About How Statutes Are to Be Construed," *Vanderbilt Law Review* 3 (1950): 395–406.

[5]Scalia opposed the use of legislative history to establish intent and co-authored a book listing the canons of interpretation, many with Latin names that sound like Harry Potter spells (e.g., *Noscitur a sociis*, or "a word is known by the company it keeps"). Scalia recognized 57 such canons, but some are not widely accepted and many have opposing canons (counter-spells).

which has distinguished his rulings from the other conservative Justices. As Justice Kagan phrased it when discussing Scalia's legacy, "we're all textualists now."[6] But even a focus on "the text, the whole text, and nothing but the text" does not solve all the disagreements. How much ambiguity in the language is there? And how should we resolve a meaning that is unclear? In *Bostock*, three dissenting Justices favored "by what Congress intended it to mean at the time," but a majority of six Justices, led by Neil Gorsuch, said "by the specific textual language" regardless of where it leads.

Native rights. Another major case that revolves around statutory interpretation focuses on Native land claims, and again Justice Gorsuch resolved the question by applying his textual standard. *McGirt v. Oklahoma* focuses on congressional treaties with the Muscogee (Creek) Nation, who were removed from their original territory in the southeastern United States and moved along the Trail of Tears in the 1830s to a new Indian Territory. Over the intervening time, that land—including the city of Tulsa and many other towns—became what most Americans believed was under the government of the State of Oklahoma. But is it?

Carol Nackenoff and Natasha Markov-Riss explain in Chapter 10 how the controversy revolves around whether congressional treaties mean, as Chief Justice Roberts phrases it in the dissent, that "unbeknownst to anyone for the past century, a huge swathe of Oklahoma is actually a Creek Indian reservation."[7] As in *Bostock* on the Civil Rights Act, Gorsuch rules that we must rely on the text alone. In a ruling that surprised many commentators, he writes that "On the far end of the Trail of Tears was a promise," and "we hold the government to its word" that the reservations would be maintained. Because "wishes are not laws... If Congress wishes to withdraw its promises, it must say so."[8] From the perspective of the four dissenters, interpreting Congress' purpose as

---

See Scalia and Bryan Garner, *Reading Law: The Interpretation of Legal Texts* (Thomson West, 2012).

[6]Justice Elena Kagan, "The Scalia Lecture: A Dialogue with Justice Kagan on the Reading of Statutes at 8:28" (17 November 2015) https://today.law.harvard.edu/in-scalia-lecture-kagan-discusses-statutory-interpretation.

[7]*McGirt* Roberts dissent, page 1.

[8]*McGirt* decision, pages 1, 12, 42.

anything other than disestablishment of the reservation is "fantasy" given that "through an open and concerted effort, Congress did what it set out to do: transform a reservation into a State."[9] But Gorsuch and the four liberal Justices had the last word, accusing the dissenters of "ignoring the written law" for practical purposes. Gorsuch concludes that ignoring the specific text would be "the rule of the strong, not the rule of law."[10]

Public fraud. Another statutory case this year addresses the Bridge-gate controversy, in which two minions of New Jersey Governor Chris Christie punished a local mayor, Jersey-style, for not supporting their boss. When they shut down two lanes of the George Washington Bridge for several days in order to intentionally snarl traffic in Ft. Lee, NJ, was that a criminal act under federal law? A jury thought so, and so did several federal judges, but the Court unanimously disagreed. The nine Justices did not dispute that it was corrupt and bad, only whether it was illegal. As Jennifer Bowie explains in Chapter 9, the Court insists that if the Congress wishes to criminalize this sort of behavior they have to do it clearly. Prosecutors may want to extend the bounds of criminal behavior to cover abuse of political power, but they cannot until the legislature authorizes them to do so.

Immigration. This year's conflict over immigration centered on DACA, the Obama-era program that protects childhood arrivals from deportation. When the Trump administration rescinded the program, both sides agreed that one President's Department of Homeland Security could undo their predecessor's policies, *if they had done it right.* The only question was whether things had been done honestly and following the proper procedures. Under the Administrative Procedure Act (APA)—a core law guiding how federal agencies can and cannot conduct business—actions that are not fully justified can be considered "arbitrary and capricious" and hence unlawful. As John Eastman (who filed an amicus brief to the Court in this case) explains in Chapter 4, the Trump administration considered DACA to be unconstitutional and therefore easily removable, but the Court ruled that regardless of these considerations they had to comply with the correct procedures. Specifically, they had

---

[9] Roberts dissent at 22–23.
[10] *McGirt* decision at 28.

to give a full accounting of the impact the actions would have on the 700,000 DACA recipients and their families. The policy and partisan ramifications of maintaining DACA are tremendous, especially in the run-up to the 2020 presidential election, but the precedent for statutory interpretation of the strict demands of the APA (and hence the limits of presidential power) are even more far-reaching, underlining the Court's insistence that administrative corners cannot be cut by the executive branch in seeking its policy objectives.

Precedent and Reliance Interests (Immigration, Unanimous Juries, Abortion Regulation)

Two core principles of Supreme Court decision-making had deep influence this year. *Reliance interests* are the expectations, plans, and costs of those who believed the law would remain the same. In the DACA case, the Court ruled that the Department of Homeland Security "was required to assess whether there were reliance interests, determine whether they were significant, and weigh any such interests against competing policy concerns." In that sense, the Secretary of DHS "violated the Administrative Procedure Act (APA) by failing to adequately address important factors bearing on her decision."[11]

While reliance interests were the key factor in the DACA case, they were not in *McGirt*. Over one hundred years of settled expectations about the governance of the land in Oklahoma did not override the rights of the Native tribe under the Court's analysis of the treaties. Reliance interests are one factor of several that influence another core principle: *stare decisis*, or maintaining the Court's previous rulings. One of the abiding questions the Court faces is the extent to which its precedents are binding.

The ruling considered the most important "precedent on precedent" is *Casey* from 1992.[12] Not surprisingly, the doctrine on precedent came

---

[11] *DHS* decision, pages 26, 2.
[12] *Planned Parenthood of Southeastern Pennsylvania v. Casey*, 505 U.S. 833 (1992).

in the context of abortion regulation and *Roe v. Wade*. *Casey* recognizes several considerations that can justify overturning a precedent: the constitutional principle was wrong; the facts have changed; or the ruling has become unworkable in practice. A fourth consideration leans *against* overturning: strong reliance interests of those who have organized their lives in light of the ruling. What *Casey* does not clarify is how those four factors should be weighed against each other. *What if the facts have changed but there are also strong reliance interests?* Individual Justices are free to work out the conclusion for themselves in each individual case. Clearly precedent must not *always* be respected or nothing could change, but clearly it should *sometimes* be respected or the law would be an ass. Aside from those gross generalizations there is little agreement.

Precedents are not promises. Perhaps a clear example of a widely held attitude toward precedent was expressed in a headline by the editorial board of *The Washington Post*: "The Supreme Court should respect precedent. But this one decision it was right to overturn."[13] Of course we should respect precedent, unless I think it is wrong. Precedent for thee but not for me may be the standard operating procedure in the current day, not just for journalists but even for many of the Justices of the Court. Both ideological sides of the Court have made clear that precedent is a secondary consideration. Justice Ginsburg on the Left has written that "*stare decisis* is not an inexorable command" and therefore "I would not cling to those ill-advised decisions."[14] Justice Thomas on the Right has also been clear that "when faced with a demonstrably wrong precedent, my rule is simple: We should not follow it."[15] The true test of the power of precedent—would a Justice follow it rather than their own strongly held view?—is rarely met. The exceptions may be found in the current center of the Court, populated by the more pragmatic Elena Kagan on the Left and perhaps surprisingly John Roberts on the Right.[16]

---

[13]23 April 2020 www.washingtonpost.com/opinions/the-supreme-court-should-respect-precedent-but-this-is-one-decision-they-were-right-to-overturn.

[14]*Gamble v US* (2019) Ginsburg dissent, pages 7, 2. See *SCOTUS 2019* Chapter 5 by Rory Little.

[15]*Gamble* Thomas concurrence, page 9.

[16]Both Kagan and Roberts were the most likely this term to join with the other ideological bloc, Kagan casting a conservative vote in 30% of cases and Roberts a liberal vote in 38% of cases. (See Chapter 15.)

The Court's clearest discussion of precedent this year came in *Ramos* on unanimous juries (the subject of the *Washington Post* editorial), while the most dramatic application of precedent came in *June Medical* on abortion regulation.

Nonunanimous juries. Evangelisto Ramos was convicted of murder by a 10-2 vote of a Louisiana jury. Two US states, Louisiana and Oregon, allowed nonunanimous juries to render guilty verdicts, even for major crimes (as do Puerto Rico and the US military under the Uniform Code of Military Justice). The right to a jury in a criminal trial is guaranteed under the Sixth Amendment, but does a jury that can decide guilt with a nonunanimous verdict count as a real jury?

The Court had already ruled on this issue in a case called *Apodaca v. Oregon* almost fifty years ago.[17] At that time the Justices decided that nonunanimous juries do not violate the Constitution: the core of the jury right is control of convictions by peers rather than government officials, but not the unanimity of the jury. As David Klein explains in Chapter 12, this year the Court overturned that ruling, striking down nonunanimous verdicts as a violation of the Sixth Amendment. Six Justices voted to overturn the precedent, while three (Alito, Kagan, and Roberts) argued that *stare decisis* should prevail in this situation. Neither precedent nor reliance interests were strong enough to sway the Court.[18]

Abortion regulation. The *Apodaca* precedent was from 1972. Which is very close to 1973. And the well-known precedent from 1973 is of course *Roe v. Wade*. In one of the most divisive controversies this year, the Court struck down the recent Louisiana abortion regulations. The holding of *Roe v. Wade* protecting a fundamental right to abortion was not officially on the table, but its constitutional theory of a broad right of liberty found in the Due Process Clause of the Fourteenth Amendment always is. The counterargument supported by at least four members of the current Court is that no such clear right exists in the language of

---

[17]406 U.S. 404 (1972).

[18]The reliance interests of the state prosecutors are quite large (Alito calls them "massive and entirely reasonable reliance," dissent at 26). It is unclear if the many nonunanimous convictions in the past will be reversed or if the ruling only means that states may no longer continue the practice in the future. The Court has already accepted a case for next year on whether *Ramos* is retro-active (*Edwards v. Vannoy*).

the Constitution, which leaves the question of abortion regulation as a democratic decision for the voters of each state. Louisiana decided to regulate abortion providers to the point that few can survive. Are these rules a legitimate medical regulation or a clear block to a protected right? Four Justices said it was the first; four said it was the second. Chief Justice Roberts said that if this were a new case, he would agree with the conservatives that the Louisiana law does not violate the Constitution, but because the Court ruled otherwise four years ago (before Justice Kennedy was replaced by Justice Kavanaugh), he was upholding the precedent and striking down the regulation.

As Gerald Rosenberg explains in Chapter 7 on *June Medical Services v. Russo*, Roberts relies on precedent to cast the deciding vote: "*Stare decisis* instructs us to treat like cases alike. The result in this case is controlled by our decision four years ago invalidating a nearly identical Texas law."[19] It's just that simple: we already decided this. Does this mean he would also take the same position on *Roe*? Hard to say. All of the Justices believe that *sometimes*, based on *some criteria*, precedent must be overruled. But the times and criteria differ among the Justices. In *Ramos* neither precedent nor reliance interests won the day, while in *June Medical* precedent played a decisive role.

Criminal Prosecution and the Rights of Defendants (Unanimous Juries, Public Fraud, Insanity Defense)

The constitutional and statutory standards for criminal prosecution were highlighted in three major cases this year. *Ramos* on unanimous juries and *Kelly* on public fraud expanded the protections of criminal defendants. The third case is *Kahler v. Kansas* on the insanity defense. The legislature of Kansas removed a large chunk of the insanity defense from its criminal law on the grounds that many claims of insanity were bogus. Was that a violation of due process guaranteed by the Constitution? In contrast to the two pro-defendant rulings this year, in regard to the

---

[19] *June Medical* Roberts concurrence at 16.

insanity defense the Court allowed states to restrict the claims of defendants. The heart of the question is about facts: Can Kansas redefine the nature of insanity within its borders, or does it have to accept the facts about insanity shared by the rest of the nation?

Social Facts and Federalism (*Kahler, Ramos, June Medical, Bostock*)

Whether Kansas can take a different view of insanity than the rest of the nation is essentially a question of social facts: not what is *right*, but what is *real*. The Court often has to determine prevailing social realities that are part of a constitutional conflict: Is a fetus a person? Is a minor the same as an adult as a holder of rights? Is racism still blocking minority voting in the Southern states?[20] In *Kahler v. Kansas* on the insanity defense, the factual question is about the boundaries of mental illness.

As Julia Bess Frank and Mark Graber explain in Chapter 8, the venerable *M'Naghten* rule from 1843 established a baseline of who we consider to be insane and hence not legally responsible for their actions. However, the scholarly and public perceptions of insanity have changed dramatically (several times) between *M'Naghten* and *Kahler*. The most commonly accepted legal definition of insanity includes that someone who does not comprehend the rightness or wrongness of their actions is insane. Kansas (and also to some degree Alaska, Idaho, Montana, and Utah) say the reality is different, and that insanity is really grounded in *intent*, which means that someone who cannot understand the moral implications of their actions *but still intends to do it* is not insane and can be convicted of murder, as James Kahler was for intentionally killing his ex-wife, two daughters, and mother-in-law. The three dissenters (led by Justice Stephen Breyer) say that the Court's ruling is constitutionally wrong *because it is factually wrong*. But in the view of six of the Justices,

---

[20]These are the core factual questions in *Roe* (1973), *Morse v. Frederick*, commonly known as the "Bong Hits 4 Jesus" case (2007), and *Shelby County* (2013), just to name a few.

the empirical reality is not clear. The facts are disputable because the "uncertainties about the human mind loom large."[21]

Perhaps more important than the answer to any single question about prevailing realities is the broader problem of *Who gets to decide?* The Court for the whole nation? Individual state legislatures for their own parts of the country? The Court ruled in *Kahler* that when facts are uncertain, states can decide for themselves.

This relates to the concept of *federalism*: the constitutional principle that states have a large degree of autonomous authority, or as the Tenth Amendment describes it, whatever powers are not specifically allotted to the national government are held at the state level as the default. That means that states can legislate many controversial policies, but perhaps also some contested realities. The *Kahler* ruling upholds what could be called the *federalism of facts*, a new and influential doctrinal development this year. How far the federalism of facts extends—to which realities at what times—is unclear, but at the very least the current Court believes it applies to the nature of insanity.

On the subject of facts and lies, the Court staked out new territory this year in the DACA ruling in regard to the judicial judgment of honesty. Accusations of lying in politics are nothing new, but the argument that the Supreme Court should judge the veracity of public officials and throw out otherwise legitimate actions as a violation of administrative law if they lie is very new indeed. In the Census case last year, Roberts called out the administration for not telling the truth: he used the terms "pretext" and "contrived," which are legalese for lying.[22] This year the accusation was not falsehood per se, but instead not telling the *whole* truth when the administration failed to honestly consider the interests of the DACA recipients. The ruling refers to these "conspicuous" facts as mandatory for administrative consideration.[23] But which facts are obvious and important in the current day is anything but clear. The legal argument—and now Supreme Court doctrine—that failing to

---

[21] *Kahler* decision, page 8.
[22] Roberts also states that "the evidence tells a story that does not match the explanation," and "what was provided was more of a distraction." See *SCOTUS 2019* Chapter 3 by Brett Curry.
[23] *DHS* decision, page 20.

tell the truth or the whole truth is grounds for striking down government action under honesty review has tremendous ramifications.

Citizenship (DACA, *McGirt, Hernández*)

One of the things we must continually define is citizenship. In an immigrant and settler society not based on shared ethnicity or a long-standing historical culture, it is not always easy to define who is a member of the body politic. Citizenship defines who is (and is not) a recognized holder of rights and a legitimate claimer of obligations from other citizens.[24] The concept of citizenship influenced several major decisions this year, including the rulings on DACA, Native rights, and especially noncitizen rights in *Hernández v. Mesa*.

One way of understanding the DACA case is that it highlights the question of what obligations to fair treatment are due to residents who are noncitizens? One side claims that residency and the implicit promises of past policy create strong reliance interests that must be taken into account, while the other side maintains that illegal residency and policies that explicitly deny the generation of reliance interests do no such thing. In the *McGirt* case the controversy focuses on members of a separate nation with whom the United States was once at war, but later incorporated into the Republic as citizens. One of the dissent's major arguments is that the Congress made the Creek Indians US citizens in 1901, which altered their previous status as primarily citizens of a nation with whom the United States had treaties. What obligations are due to them based on historical treaties and treatment?

Hernández v. Mesa asks a clear question about the politics of the US–Mexican border: When do rights apply to noncitizens? One could

---

[24]In *US v. Verdugo-Urquidez*, 494 U.S. 259 (1990) the Court defined "the people" referenced in the Preamble and who hold constitutional rights recognized by the Bill of Rights as "a class of persons who are part of a national community or who have otherwise developed sufficient connection with this country to be considered part of that community." Citizenship relates directly to a long-run debate over the degree of constitutional protection: If the protections of the Bill of Rights are incorporated under the Due Process Clause of the Fourteenth Amendment they apply to all "persons," but if incorporated under the Privileges and Immunities Clause they apply to the smaller group of "citizens." See the discussion in Chapter 12 on the *Ramos* ruling.

imagine a continuum from the highest claim to being a holder of constitutional rights (a US citizen on US soil) to the lowest claim (a foreign national on a battlefield shooting at US soldiers, who holds zero due process rights before being killed by the US government). But what are the situations in between? In *Hernández* the question is about a noncitizen on foreign soil but as close as possible to US soil as one can get (meters away from the border). The Court deeply disagreed on his status as a rights holder. As Paul Collins and Rebecca Hamlin discuss in Chapter 6, the Court ruled that a Mexican national killed on Mexican soil by a US Border Patrol agent on the US side does not hold due process rights under the US Constitution.

The second constitutional question in *Hernández* is about the available recourse for rights violations. The Bill of Rights is clear about what the government cannot do, but is utterly silent about what happens if government agents do those things anyway. The usual remedy is to stop doing it, but as the Court noted in the *Bivens* decision in 1971, "power, once granted, does not disappear like a magic gift when it is wrongfully used."[25] If someone is harmed unconstitutionally can they sue for restitution? Whether officials like Border Patrol agents (or police) have immunity against civil lawsuits will no doubt be an important political and constitutional issue in the coming years.

Elections (*Chiafalo* on "Faithless Electors")

The question of citizenship leads us to the question of elections. The disputes in the DACA, *McGirt*, and *Hernández* cases include explicit or implicit questions about who counts—who gets to be represented in our system, either as holders of rights or as voters in elections. Beyond the question of *who* gets to be represented are the debates over *how* they are represented. One of the recurring controversies in American politics is about the Electoral College, our unusual and little-understood system of presidential selection. In Chapter 3 on *Chiafalo v. Washington*, Justin Dyer and Erin Hawley discuss the ruling on the problem of faithless

---

[25] *Bivens v. Six Unknown Named Agents*, 403 U.S. 388 (1971) at 392.

electors—those cogs in the electoral machinery who refuse to do what most Americans think is their job of recording the electoral winner of their state, instead insisting on voting for someone else.

In a rare show of unity, both the originalist and living constitutionalist Justices came together in this unanimous decision to uphold the power of states to determine how electoral votes will be cast. Justice Kagan wrote the ruling, which seems to uphold both federalism and textualism. In the oral arguments in May, she had asked a piercing question: "Suppose that I read the Constitution and I find that it just doesn't say anything about this subject … What should I then do and why?"[26] In the decision she observed that "whether by choice or accident, the Framers did not reduce their thoughts about electors' discretion to the printed page." Because the text merely says that each state will appoint electors "in such Manner as the Legislature thereof may direct" (Article II, §1), this gives individual states great latitude. If a state has decided that popular democracy within its borders should be the law of the land—as all US states have done over the last two centuries, in either winner-take-all or proportional representation, as they see fit—then they can do so without hindrance. She concludes that "the Constitution's text and the Nation's history both support allowing a State to enforce an elector's pledge to support his party's nominee— and the state voters' choice—for President." Now, as from almost the beginning of the Republic, "No independent electors need apply."[27]

Separation of Powers and the Rivalry Between the Congress and the Presidency

The separation of powers—a core feature of constitutional government designed to limit the abuse of authority—is a recurring concern of the Court. When it comes to the long-standing rivalry between the Congress and the Presidency, the current partisan polarization was bound to lead

---

[26] *Colorado Department of State v. Baca* oral arguments transcript page 50.
[27] *Chiafalo* decision, pages 13, 9, 15.

to constitutional disputes over their competing powers. Two controversies this year focus on the control of the federal bureaucracy and on the subpoenas of the President.

When reformers (led by Senator Elizabeth Warren) set up the Consumer Finance Protection Bureau to shield ordinary citizens from powerful banks, they made the head of the CFPB unremovable by the President. But as Howard Schweber explains in Chapter 13, this runs directly into the argument that the Constitution gives each branch of the federal government control over its own sphere, including an executive branch agency set up by the President's critics. The Court ruled in favor of presidential power over the federal bureaucracy, making the head of the CFPB (and potentially other agencies) removable at the discretion of the President. This bolsters a controversial constitutional doctrine known as the *unitary executive theory*, which holds that the President has full accountability and control of executive branch activities, even ones for which there is an argument for independent or nonpartisan judgment (such as the Justice Department or in this case the CFPB).

Cornell Clayton and Joseph Bolton describe the subpoena controversies in Chapter 14. *Trump v. Mazars* asks whether the Congress has the authority to issue subpoenas for the President's financial records, while *Trump v. Vance* asks the same question about the authority of local district attorneys investigating possible criminal behavior. One backdrop is the long-standing attempt by Democratic politicians to gain access to Donald Trump's tax returns (which every other presidential candidate of the major parties going back to Dwight Eisenhower has made public). The other backdrop is of course the investigation into allegations that the Trump campaign colluded with foreign governments during the 2016 campaign and the impeachment proceedings brought by the House of Representatives in December of 2019. The first Article of Impeachment was about the infamous phone call with the President of the Ukraine, but the second Article of Impeachment was for resisting congressional requests for information. The acquittal in the Senate did not end the subpoenas for the President's tax records, issued by several committees of the House of Representatives.

Chief Justice Roberts wrote the Court's ruling in both cases. In the congressional case he notes that this dispute "is the first of its kind to reach this Court."[28] With the unanimous support of the other Justices, Roberts rejected the extreme positions and advanced a balanced approach. Presidents, he said, are not immune from congressional subpoenas, but they must be related directly to ongoing legislation and justified in clear terms, which these requests were not.[29] Quoting Alexander Hamilton in *Federalist* #71, Roberts concludes that "without limits on its subpoena powers, Congress could 'exert an imperious controul' over the Executive Branch and aggrandize itself at the President's expense, just as the Framers feared."[30]

In the case of local prosecutors issuing subpoenas for the President's records, again this is a new question for the Court. The core constitutional issue is whether the President is absolutely immune from the issuance of subpoenas while in office. The answer provided by all nine Justices is No. There is surprising unanimity that "the President is neither absolutely immune from state criminal subpoenas seeking his private papers nor entitled to a heightened standard of need" before a subpoena can be issued. However, the President can still "argue that compliance with a particular subpoena would impede his constitutional duties" and if he is persuasive, then "at that point, a court should use its inherent authority to quash or modify the subpoena."[31] Hence the case must be remanded back to the lower courts for further proceedings (which will no doubt stretch for some months) before a final decision can be reached. Whether further attempts at presidential subpoenas—of this President or others—will succeed or fail based on this standard will play out in the future.

---

[28] *Trump v. Mazars* opinion, page 10.

[29] The two 'dissenters' are conservative Justices Alito and Thomas who take the position that the subpoenas are even more suspect and lacking in foundation.

[30] *Trump v. Mazars* decision, page 16. It is important to note that this applies to congressional subpoenas issued under the normal course of Congress' legislative and oversight duties, not to subpoenas issued during impeachment proceedings. That question has not been resolved.

[31] *Trump v. Vance* decision, pages 21, 20–21.

Religious Liberty (*Espinoza, Lady of Guadalupe*, and *Little Sisters*)

In a year with prominent abortion and gay rights cases we also have a set of religious liberty cases. The Court has considered many times whether various programs by state governments can include or exclude religious institutions without violating the Constitution. Similar controversies address whether religious organizations and schools are exempt from antidiscrimination laws for many of their employees (under what is known as the "ministerial exception") and whether the mandate under the Affordable Care Act (Obamacare) requiring employers to pay for contraception applies to religious organizations. The Court has ruled in favor of religious liberty claims several times in recent years, and as Kevin Pybas discusses in Chapter 5, did so again in this trifecta of rulings.

When tensions flare between the right to practice religion without state interference (the Free Exercise Clause of the First Amendment) and the right to be free of religious imposition or favoritism by the state (the Establishment Clause), the protections of Free Exercise have been coming out ahead of the limits of Establishment.[32] In *Espinoza* the Court ruled that "A State need not subsidize private education. But once a State decides to do so, it cannot disqualify some private schools solely because they are religious."[33] While many of the religion rulings of the Court in recent years have been 7-2 (with Justices Breyer and Kagan joining the conservatives), *Espinoza* was decided 5-4, illustrating the limit of the liberal agreement with religious liberty claims when it comes to state funding of religious education.

---

[32]The recent religious liberty rulings include *Hobby Lobby* (2014), *Trinity Lutheran* (2017), *Masterpiece Cakeshop* (2018), and *American Legion* (2019). See *SCOTUS 2018* Chapter 2 on *Masterpiece Cakeshop* by Stephen Engel and *SCOTUS 2019* Chapter 2 on *American Legion* by Ronald Kahn and Gerard D'Emilio.

[33]*Espinoza* decision at 20. While *Espinoza* and *Lady of Guadalupe* focus on the *constitutional interpretation* of the First Amendment, the third religious liberty case is more about *statutory interpretation*: *Little Sisters of the Poor* focuses on the meaning of several pieces of major congressional legislation, including the Affordable Care Act of 2010 (ACA), the Administrative Procedure Act of 1946 (APA), and the Religious Freedom Restoration Act of 1993 (RFRA).

Guns (*New York Rifle & Pistol*)

It has been a decade since the Court recognized a fundamental right for individual citizens to bear arms. That case was *MacDonald v. Chicago*, from the city with the highest total number of gun deaths in the nation, following *District of Columbia v. Heller* from the nation's capital. Since that time, the looming question has been what sort of restrictions would be considered constitutional. As Austin Sarat explains in Chapter 11, the Court was poised to make a major ruling on the New York City regulation that limited legal gun owners from transporting firearms to any location within or outside the city aside from a small number of designated firing ranges. Before the Court could rule on whether this was permissible under the Second Amendment, the case shifted in character because the city withdrew the regulation. The Court had to decide if the case was fully moot—no longer a live controversy—or whether they should still rule on the remaining smaller issues or the larger constitutional questions. Though the Court ruled that this case was moot, the controversy about the meaning and limits of the Second Amendment will no doubt continue in future cases.

Conclusion: Ideology and the Major Trends of the Year

Many of the major cases this year reflected the partisan controversies of the Trump presidency (subpoenas, faithless electors, immigration, executive powers). Chief Justice Roberts issued a rare statement upbraiding Democratic Senator Chuck Schumer, the Minority Leader of the Senate, for his comments about the conservative Justices in a speech on the New York gun case.[34] This was preceded by an amicus ("friend of the

---

[34]"Senator Schumer referred to two Members of the Court by name and said he wanted to tell them that 'You have released the whirlwind, and you will pay the price. You will not know what hit you if you go forward with these awful decisions.' Justices know that criticism comes with the territory, but threatening statements of this sort from the highest levels of government are not only inappropriate, they are dangerous" (4 March 2020) statement of Chief Justice John Roberts.

Court") brief in the same case by Senator Sheldon Whitehouse (D. Rhode Island), in which he threatened that if the Court did not dismiss the case, the Senate would have to consider adding more Justices in an attempt to shift its partisan balance, otherwise known as "Court packing." This document quickly earned the nickname of "the enemy of the Court" brief.[35] In a presidential election year, several decisions have made the Court more central to the campaign than usual, especially the abortion and LGBT cases, as well as the DACA and Trump subpoena rulings.

With all of this in mind, one might have expected a deeply and predictably divided year of many 5-4 decisions along ideological lines. However, as Lawrence Baum explains in Chapter 15, there were far fewer of those kinds of rulings and far more ideological cross-overs than one might expect. Led by Roberts and Gorsuch, some of the conservatives allied with the liberals in several major rulings. Chief Justice Roberts wrote major rulings expressing the Court's view for himself and the liberals as well as himself and the conservatives. Only Roberts was in the majority in 14 of the 16 major rulings discussed in this volume (writing five of those opinions himself). This was clearly Roberts' year.

It was clearly not the conservatives' year to the degree we might expect from a majority of five Justices. A substantial number of liberal outcomes balanced the conservative ones. The Court struck down abortion regulations while also expanding religious liberty. The Justices upheld DACA while also limiting lawsuits by noncitizens. They upheld the principle that the presidency is not above the requirements of legal process, but also limited the power of Congress to demand records from a sitting President. They expanded Native rights and protections for LGBT citizens. Among the many substantive rulings, the Court also broke new doctrinal ground in honesty review and the federalism of facts. The role of textualism as a means of interpretation continues to be deeply influential. Reliance interests are a core concern, even as precedent is wobbly. The separation of powers remains a powerful constitutional doctrine and the unitary executive theory received a boost. It was quite a year to watch,

---

[35]See Austin Sarat, "Democrats Turn a Venerable Legal Tool into a Declaration of War," TheConversation.com (26 August 2019).

with every indication that the string of landmark cases will continue in the future as the Court continues to face major disputes over citizenship and immigration, presidential power, religious liberty (especially when it veers into conflict with LGBT rights, which is to say when *Bostock* meets *Espinoza*), the recurring debates over the statutory interpretation of the Affordable Care Act, the separation of powers, guns, and restitution for the use of force, and among many other controversies.

2

Bostock v. Clayton County on LGBT Employment Discrimination

Julie Novkov

On June 15, 2020, the Supreme Court decided *Bostock v. Clayton County*, resolving whether Title VII of the Civil Rights Act of 1964 protects American workers against discrimination based on sexual orientation and gender identity. In a 6-3 ruling authored by Justice Neil Gorsuch, the Court ruled in favor of the plaintiffs in a landmark for LGBT rights.

Advocates for LGBTQ equality hailed the ruling as a surprise victory. The Court appeared to be tilting in a more conservative direction after swing Justice Anthony Kennedy's retirement in 2018 and his replacement with Federalist Society stalwart Brett Kavanaugh. Justice Gorsuch, President Trump's first Court appointee, was also a reliable conservative vote in most cases, but played a pivotal role in this ruling.

This essay reviews the claims, and then, as Justice Gorsuch does, considers the language and history of Title VII's prohibition against discrimination on the basis of sex. It summarizes Justice Gorsuch's broad use of textualism to reach the outcome and briefly addresses the dissents.

J. Novkov (✉)
University at Albany, SUNY, Albany, NY, USA

© The Author(s) 2021
M. Marietta (ed.), *SCOTUS 2020*,
https://doi.org/10.1007/978-3-030-53851-4_2

The chapter concludes by noting that while *Bostock* answers many questions, the majority opinion explicitly reserves an important consideration for a later day.

The Three Lawsuits

The ruling resolved appeals in three related cases: *Bostock, Altitude Express, Inc. v. Zarda,* and *R. G. and G. R. Harris Funeral Homes, Inc. v. Equal Employment Opportunity Commission.* The Court frequently grants review when two or more of the geographic judicial circuits have reached opposite outcomes on a national question. These cases produced split rulings in the Eleventh, Second, and Sixth Circuits interpreting Title VII's coverage.

The first of the trio was *Zarda v. Altitude Express.* In the summer of 2010, Donald Zarda worked as an instructor in a Long Island skydiving business. As part of the training process, "he regularly participated in tandem skydives, strapped hip-to-hip" with clients.[1] After such an episode in a tandem skydive, Zarda was fired after a female client complained that he had outed himself to her, intending to allay her (and her boyfriend's) concerns about the physical contact. He contacted the EEOC, claiming that he had been terminated on the basis of both sexual orientation and sex. He filed suit in September 2010. Fearing that the controversy over his firing would make it impossible for him to find future skydiving employment, he turned to the extreme sport of BASE jumping (which involves jumping off cliffs or fixed structures with a parachute or wing suit), and lost his life in an accident in 2014. His sister and his partner maintained the suit on behalf of his estate.

Aimee Stephens was hired by R. G. and G. R. Harris Funeral Homes in 2007 and became the Funeral Director in 2008. When hired, she presented and worked as a man. On July 31, 2013, Stephens informed the owner and operator of the business, Thomas Rost, that she intended to have sex reassignment surgery after living and working full-time as a woman for a year. She proposed returning to work after her summer

---

[1] *Zarda v. Altitude Express, Inc.,* 883 F.3d 100 (2018).

vacation in women's business attire. Just before her vacation, Rost fired her, explaining that his religious beliefs prevented him from acknowledging or employing Stephens as a woman. The Equal Employment Opportunity Commission sued on her behalf. In early 2018, the Sixth Circuit ruled that discrimination against individuals on the basis of transgender or transitioning status was actionable under Title VII.[2] Despite her decline from kidney disease, Stephens continued to speak out on transgender issues, attending oral arguments on her case in October 2019. She died in May, prior to the Court's ruling in *Bostock*.

Gerald Bostock began working for Clayton County, near Atlanta, Georgia, in 2003 as the Child Welfare Services Coordinator. In January 2013, he became involved with a local gay recreational softball league, promoting his agency to league members as a volunteer opportunity. In June, he was fired for "conduct unbecoming of a County employee."[3] Bostock sued, but the Eleventh Circuit Court of Appeals ruled against him, finding that Title VII did not bar discrimination based on sexual orientation.[4] While he was able to find employment as a mental health counselor at an Atlanta-area hospital, he maintained his claim, in part because he believes that his firing "sent a negative message to all LGBTQ people in Clayton County—especially LGBTQ youth."[5]

Title VII and Sex Discrimination

Congress enacted Title VII in 1964 as a part of the landmark Civil Rights Act. The legislation was aimed primarily at racial discrimination, and the provision addressing sex was not a part of the law as originally drafted. It came in as an amendment proposed by Democratic Representative Howard Smith, a known opponent of civil rights. Smith's gambit has

---

[2] *Equal Employment Opportunity Commission v. R. G. & G. R. Harris Funeral Homes, Inc.*, No. 16–2424 (6th Cir. 2018).

[3] *Bostock v. Clayton County* (N.D. Georgia, 2016) at 3–4.

[4] *Bostock v. Clayton County Board of Commissioners*, No. 17–13801 (11th Cir. 2018).

[5] Trudy Ring, "Fired After Joining a Gay Softball Team, This Man Is Fighting Back," *The Advocate* (4 October 2019).

been portrayed as a failed attempt to take down the legislation by incorporating sex as a poison pill. The deeper story is more complicated. The National Woman's Party, which had been pushing for an equal rights amendment since the 1920s, supported amending the civil rights bill and worked to find allies in Congress. Three Representatives—Smith, Katherine St. George, and Martha Griffiths—agreed to introduce the amendment. While Smith opposed the entire bill, "Griffiths felt that Smith's sponsorship would insure at least a hundred Southern votes."[6] When the legislation went to the Senate, the National Federation of Business and Professional Women rallied behind it.

The Act makes it an "unlawful employment practice for an employer … to discriminate against any individual with respect to his compensation, terms, conditions, or privileges or employment, because of such individual's … sex."[7] Aggrieved persons used the new legislation to bring claims at the Equal Employment Opportunity Commission, as the new federal agency developed its interpretations of sex discrimination.[8]

The Supreme Court, often following the EEOC's lead, initially traced an uncertain path. The first Supreme Court case addressing sex was *Phillips v. Martin Marietta Corporation* in 1971. Martin Marietta had refused to hire Phillips because she had young children, and claimed that since 75–80% of the hired employees in the position she sought were women, sex discrimination could not be established. In a short per curiam ruling, the Court allowed the suit to proceed.[9]

The Court established sex as a protected class under the Constitution in the 1976 landmark case, *Craig v. Boren*.[10] However, in the same year, the Court ruled that an employer's denial of insurance benefits for pregnancy when other conditions were covered did not constitute sex discrimination under Title VII.[11] In 1978, the Court ruled that a

---

[6]Jo Freeman, "How Sex Got into Title VII: Persistent Opportunism as a Maker of Public Policy," *Law & Inequality: A Journal of Theory and Practice* 9, no. 2 (n.d.): 175.

[7]"Title VII," Pub. L. No. 88–352, title VII, § 703 (1964).

[8]Jennifer Woodward, "Making Rights Work: Legal Mobilization at the Agency Level," *Law and Society Review* 49, no. 3 (2015): 703.

[9]*Phillips v. Martin Marietta Corporation*, 400 U.S. 542 (1971).

[10]429 U.S. 190 (1976).

[11]*Geduldig v. Aiello*, 417 U.S. 484 (1974); *General Elec. Co. v. Gilbert*, 429 U.S. 125 (1976).

public utility employer could not require women to contribute larger sums to their pension funds than men because on average, women tended to live longer than men.[12] The same year, Congress amended Title VII to mandate that discrimination on the basis of pregnancy was sex discrimination.[13]

In the 1980s, the Justices expanded Title VII's definition of sex discrimination. In 1979, Catharine MacKinnon laid the groundwork for the EEOC's guidelines incorporating sexual harassment as a form of prohibited sex discrimination, a standard that the Court endorsed in 1986.[14] And in 1989, the Court allowed a suit to proceed in which the plaintiff, Ann Hopkins, was denied a partnership in an accounting firm because she did not conform to their expectations of gendered behavior.[15] While not every Title VII case addressing sex resulted in expansion, the Court interpreted the meaning of discrimination because of sex by looking beyond understandings of what might have raised concerns in the 1960s. However, the path regarding sexual orientation and gender identity was more complicated.

Title VII, Sexual Orientation, and Gender Identity

Constitutional analyst William Eskridge notes that "Title VII in 1964 would not have been applied to ensure a liberal workplace for 'homosexuals' or 'transsexuals,' for those Americans were, literally, considered psychopaths, criminals, and enemies of the people."[16] A few unsuccessful suits sought statutory and constitutional protections for lesbians and gay men in the 1970s, including the Supreme Court's summary rejection of

---

[12] *City of Los Angeles Dep't of Water & Power v. Manhart*, 435 U.S. 702 (1978).

[13] "Pregnancy Discrimination Act," Pub. L. No. 95–555 (1978).

[14] Augustus Cochran III, *Sexual Harassment and the Law: The Mechelle Vinson Case* (Lawrence, KS: University Press of Kansas, 2004).

[15] *Price Waterhouse v. Hopkins*, 490 U.S. 228 (1989).

[16] William Eskridge, "Title VII's Statutory History and the Sex Discrimination Argument for LGBT Workplace Protections," *Yale Law Journal* 127 (2017): 336.

the first attempt to legitimize same-sex marriage in 1972. Shortly afterward, the Fifth Circuit's courts rejected Title VII protection for a man fired because he presented himself in an effeminate fashion and another because he was gay.[17]

Transgender issues simmered as well. In 1984, the Seventh Circuit considered the appeal of Eastern Airlines involving a suit by a pilot, hired in 1968 as Kenneth Ulane and fired in 1981 as Karen Frances Ulane. Ulane transitioned fully in 1980, but Eastern knew nothing of her situation until she returned to work after surgery, triggering her dismissal. The circuit court found that Title VII did not incorporate discrimination on this basis.[18]

While the Supreme Court acknowledged sexual harassment as a prohibited practice under Title VII in the 1980s, same-sex sexual harassment and harassment for being gay or lesbian generated conflicting rulings.[19] The Court resolved the confusion in 1998. In a landmark ruling for a unanimous Court delivered in an opinion by Justice Antonin Scalia, the Justices found that Title VII allowed for liability for same-sex sexual harassment.[20]

Over the next two decades, the federal courts grappled with further questions beyond employment. In 2003, the Court ruled that states could not prohibit private consensual homosexual intimacy, and over the next twelve years, the struggle for same-sex marriage unfolded, ultimately culminating in *Obergefell v. Hodges'* extension of same-sex marriage rights to all couples nationwide.[21]

In 2014, the Obama-era EEOC interpreted Title VII to cover discrimination based on sexual orientation and gender identity. The guidance followed EEOC rulings that recognized both forms of discrimination as sufficient allegations to support EEOC action.[22] The guidelines and the conflicting circuit court rulings set up the Supreme Court confrontation.

---

[17]Ibid. at 353.

[18]*Ulane v. Eastern Airlines*, 742 F.2d 1081 (7th Cir. 1984).

[19]Jack Harrison, "Because of Sex," *Loyola L.A. Law Review* 51 (2018): 111–112.

[20]*Oncale v. Sundowner Offshore Services, Inc.*, 523 U.S. 75 (1998).

[21]*Lawrence v. Texas*, 539 U.S. 558 (2003); *Obergefell v. Hodges*, 576 U.S. 644 (2015).

[22]"Preventing Discrimination Against Lesbian, Gay, Bisexual or Transgender Workers," Title VII, 29 CFR 1601, 29 CFR Part 1614 § (2014).

The *Bostock* Case

In April 2019, the Court granted certiorari in the three cases. Because the cases enabled the Court to issue a single ruling addressing the issues comprehensively, the Court consolidated them for briefing and oral arguments under *Bostock*. US Solicitor General Noel Francisco participated in the oral argument on the employers' side, as the Trump Administration had rejected the Obama Administration's position on these questions.

In his opinion for the Court, Justice Gorsuch explained the question as "whether an employer can fire someone simply for being homosexual or transgender," explaining that sex is an inextricable element of discrimination on these grounds. While Title VII's framers would not have anticipated this development, "the limits of the drafters' imagination supply no reason to ignore the law's demands."[23]

Justice Gorsuch presented his reasoning as a straightforward exercise of textual analysis. He began with "the ordinary public meaning of [a statute's] terms at the time of its enactment." While "sex" was a key term, he read the clause "because of sex" as a conceptual whole, incorporating "the 'simple' and 'traditional' standard of but-for causation." This move enabled Gorsuch to allow for liability even if other factors contributed to an employment decision: "so long as the plaintiff's sex was one but-for cause of that decision, that is enough."[24]

Gorsuch emphasized the statute's focus on individuals rather than groups. The individual focus of the law allowed analysis of questions about whether a specific person was being treated worse in some way because of their sex. Putting these two pieces together, Gorsuch explained, produces the principle that "An employer violates Title VII when it intentionally fires an employee based in part on sex."[25] And this principle encompassed discrimination against persons for being either homosexual or transgender because sex is an inextricable component of either kind of discrimination.

---

[23] *Bostock* decision, page 15.
[24] Ibid. at 4, 5–6.
[25] Ibid. at 10.

To illustrate this reasoning, Gorsuch imagined a homophobic employer hosting a party for employees and their spouses. If a model employee introduces the employer to their wife, the employee's job is only at risk if the employee is a woman (i.e., a man would not be fired for the same action that led to a woman being fired). An employer who takes adverse action against a gay or transgender employee may be incorporating both sex and some other factor to engage in discrimination, "but Title VII doesn't care."[26] For Gorsuch, this settled the matter.

From the history of the Court's expansion of sex discrimination to encompass a variety of forms, Gorsuch derived three principles. First, an employer's description of a discriminatory practice in a way that excludes reference to sex (life expectancy in *Manhart*, motherhood in *Philips*) does not enable the employer to escape liability. Second, as he had noted earlier, sex did not have to be the only factor driving an adverse employment outcome. And finally, "an employer cannot escape liability by demonstrating that it treats males and females comparably as groups."[27]

The employers' argument that Title VII did not contemplate prohibiting these types of discrimination garnered a vigorous response from Gorsuch. Rather than reading the statute as rigidly frozen in time, he advocated for the language's meaning as something that could develop. He noted that:

> to refuse enforcement just because … the parties before us happened to be unpopular at the time of the law's passage, would not only require us to abandon our role as interpreters of statues; it would tilt the scales of justice in favor of the strong or popular and neglect the promise that all persons are entitled to the benefit of the law's terms.[28]

The statute's expansion over the years further bolstered this understanding of meaning as encompassing unexpected developments.

Justice Gorsuch also resisted the employers' arguments that the consequences of the ruling would radically change employment law. He noted

---

[26]Ibid. at 11.
[27]Ibid. at 14–15.
[28]Ibid. at 28.

that questions about "sex-segregated bathrooms, locker rooms, and dress codes" were not before the Court.[29] He had more to say on the question of the potential impact of the ruling on freedom of religion, but explained that this issue was not before the Court yet.

Justice Alito's dissent

Justice Alito authored the primary dissent, which Justice Thomas joined. He objected primarily on the ground that the Court was actively legislating rather than interpreting Title VII. Accusing the majority of "deceptive" behavior, he emphasized the several failed attempts by Congress over the years to add sexual orientation and gender identity to the list of categories covered by Title VII.[30] These failures, he suggested, imply Congress' unwillingness to address discrimination on these bases, dating back to the common understanding of sex discrimination when Congress originally passed the legislation in 1964. In other words, if Congress had meant the law to include LGBT employees, they would have said so.

Alito rejected Gorsuch's form of textualism. "The Court's opinion is like a pirate ship. It sails under a textualist flag, but … actually represents … a theory of statutory interpretation that Justice Scalia excoriated—the theory that courts should 'update' old statutes so that they better reflect the current values of society."[31] He argued that the core inquiry should focus on whether Congress in 1964 had intended to incorporate sexual orientation and gender identity into the legislation, concluding that it did not. To support his argument, he analyzed the received meaning of sex in the 1960s and insisted that, in the cases before the Court, both sexual orientation and gender identity are logically distinguishable from sex.

Rebuffing Gorsuch's claim that sex is inherently part of the analysis, he explained that "it is quite possible for an employer to discriminate on those [sexual orientation or gender identity] grounds without taking the

---

[29] Ibid. at 31.
[30] Alito dissent, page 1.
[31] Ibid. at 3.

sex of an individual applicant or employee into account."[32] To Gorsuch's hypothetical office party encounter, he responded that the employer's discovery of new information about the employee's sexual orientation, not the sex of the spouse, would be the key factor in driving the negative employment outcome. In the final analysis, Alito explained, a major change to public policy should be made democratically by the legislature, not judicially by the Court.

Alito's other concern, however, went beyond the violence he believed the majority was doing to the legislative intent motivating Title VII. He anticipated "far-reaching consequences" he saw as being "virtually certain." His most dreaded implications were threats to "freedom of religion, freedom of speech, and personal privacy and safety." In addition to specific concerns about the workplace, he fretted that the ruling might "exert a gravitational pull in constitutional cases."[33]

Looking Ahead

Justice Gorsuch included an important reservation in his opinion. He noted that the Court is "deeply concerned" with maintaining free exercise of religion.[34] He underlined recent developments guarding free exercise, noting that Congress had initially included an exception in Title VII for religious organizations, that a 2012 Supreme Court ruling had prevented the application of Title VII's antidiscrimination policy to a religious organization's selection of its religious leaders, and that Congress had further protected freedom of religion through the 1993 Religious Freedom Restoration Act. Laying down a marker for a potential future dispute, Gorsuch hinted that RFRA, which he characterized as a "super statute," might override Title VII and other laws.[35]

---

[32] Ibid. at 8–9.
[33] Ibid. at 45, 53–54.
[34] *Bostock* decision, page 32.
[35] Ibid. at 32.

Justice Gorsuch's discussion follows a series of rulings bolstering such claims.[36] With this cautionary note—or perhaps invitation—in the majority opinion, further legal struggle over how much the new interpretation of Title VII will transform the American workplace looms on the horizon.

---

[36] *Burwell v. Hobby Lobby Stores*, 573 U.S. 661 (2014); *Masterpiece Cakeshop, Ltd. v. Colorado Civil Rights Commission*, 584 U.S. (2018); *Espinoza v. Montana Department of Revenue*, 591 U.S. (2020). See Chapter 5 on *Espinoza*.

3

Chiafalo v. Washington on Faithless Electors

Justin Dyer and Erin Hawley

In December 2016, when members of the Electoral College met in their respective state capitols to cast ballots for the President and Vice President of the United States, ten electors voted for candidates to whom they were not pledged. One hundred and seventy-four other electors had done the same thing in elections dating back to 1796, but the 2016 election marked the first time officials enforced state statutes penalizing presidential electors for their faithless votes.[1]

The consolidated cases of *Chiafalo v. Washington* and *Colorado Department of State v. Baca* bring to the forefront a novel constitutional question: do state governments have the authority, under the US Constitution, to enforce state statutes penalizing presidential electors for their votes in the Electoral College? According to the majority opinion authored by Justice Kagan, the answer is Yes. This conclusion, the Court

---

[1] See FairVote.org/the_electoral_college.

J. Dyer (✉) · E. Hawley
University of Missouri, Columbia, MO, USA

© The Author(s) 2021
M. Marietta (ed.), *SCOTUS 2020*,
https://doi.org/10.1007/978-3-030-53851-4_3

argued, follows from the text of Article II of the Constitution, which gives states the authority to appoint presidential electors "in such Manner as the Legislature thereof may direct."

History and Purpose of the Electoral College

As the Constitutional Convention drew to a close in the summer of 1787, New Jersey delegate David Brearley chaired a committee tasked with addressing unresolved or postponed issues. Perhaps the most significant issue the Brearley Committee tackled was the method of presidential selection. Previous proposals included choosing the national executive either by a vote of the Congress, or by a vote of either state governors or state legislatures. As Virginia delegate James Madison recorded in his notes on the proceedings of the convention, there were "objections agst. every mode that has been, or perhaps can be proposed."[2]

Delegates worried about cabal and corruption; intrigue and faction; about foreign meddling in presidential selection; about the subservience of the national executive to the electing body (whether state or national); and, finally, about the relative balance of power between small states and large states. All of this was enough for Madison to conclude, late in the summer, that the only "Option before us then lay between an appointment by Electors chosen by the people – and an immediate appointment by the people."[3]

The Brearley Committee proposed the former, and the Convention finally adopted a plan for each state to appoint a number of presidential electors equal to the state's congressional delegation. The electors must not already hold an "office of trust or profit under the United States" (a provision designed to prevent the corruption or cabal of national officeholders). These electors would then gather in their respective state capitols on a day determined by Congress to cast two ballots each for the president, which they would then sign, certify, and "transmit sealed

---

[2] *The Records of the Federal Convention of 1787*, ed. Max Farrand, 3 vols. (New Haven: Yale University Press, 1911), 2:109.

[3] Ibid., 2:110.

to the seat of government of the United States, directed to the President of the Senate." In the presence of the House and Senate, the President of the Senate would then count the signed and certified votes from the electors, and the person with the highest number of votes—provided it is a majority of the votes cast—would become President of the United States and the person with the second highest number of votes the Vice President of the United States. In the event of a tie or if the leading candidate failed to gain a majority, the election of the President would be made by the House (voting by delegation, with each state delegation having one vote) and the election of the vice-president would be by the Senate (with each Senator having one ballot).[4]

In defense of this novel electoral institution, Madison later maintained in the *Federalist Papers* that the Electoral College adequately addressed concerns about the relative balance of power between large states and small states by adopting the same compound ratio used for representation in the national legislature (with the House apportioned by population and the Senate equally apportioned among the states), and it did so while avoiding the incentive to faction and cabal that would arise from direct dependence on either the national legislature or state officials (whether executive or legislative).[5] Madison's collaborator on the *Federalist Papers*, Alexander Hamilton, similarly argued that this method of presidential selection would protect against intrigue and foreign influence by vesting the authority to select the president in a temporary body, independent of existing public officials, capable of exercising deliberation and discernment.[6] Its drafters and advocates maintained that the Electoral College was an innovative institution that addressed the unique challenges of building a government that was at once *national* (representing the nation as a whole), *federal* (giving due representation to each state or region), and *republican* (giving the people a voice in selecting and removing their leadership).

---

[4]See U.S. Constitution, Art. II, Sec. 2, Cl. 3. Only the elections of 1800 and 1824 required contingent elections for the presidency, and only the election of 1836 required a contingent election of the vice-presidency.

[5]*The Federalist* (Gideon Edition), eds. George W. Carey and James McLellan (Indianapolis: Liberty Fund, 2001), page 197.

[6]Ibid. at 352–353.

The Constitutional Arguments

The states and the presidential electors take very different views of the constitutional text, which provides that "Each State shall appoint, in such Manner as the Legislature thereof may direct, a Number of Electors" and that the Electors shall "vote by Ballot" in their representative states.[7] They also disagree over the effect of the ratification of the Twelfth Amendment, which required electors to cast one ballot for president and one ballot for vice president, and of the relevance of the contemporary understanding of the role of electors. The electors argue that the text, structure, and history of the Constitution all deny to states the power to direct the vote of electors. In contrast, the states rely on those same sources to claim that the states have that authority.

The electors argue that the original meaning of the terms "appoint," "Electors," and "vote by Ballot" in the Constitution all establish that Article II vests discretion to choose a candidate in presidential electors.[8] The electors claim that, as originally understood, the power to "appoint" is limited to the fact of appointment itself and does not include any additional power to control the appointee. Further, the Founders would have understood the term "Elector" to be a person "vested with judgment and discretion to choose."[9] The electors contend that this conclusion is confirmed by the use of the word "vote" to refer to an elector's primary constitutional duty; to vote is to choose, not merely to pass along the choices of others. In addition, the Framers specified that electors must vote "by Ballot." Voting by ballot—"a particularly secure, reliable, and objective voting method"—was adopted by the Framers as the mode "best calculated to secure a freedom of choice."[10] Finally, the electors also note that constitutional structure supports elector independence: in our federal system, a state may not control or direct the performance of a "federal function," like the election of president.

---

[7]U.S. Constitution, Art. II, Sec. 2, Cl. 2 & 3.
[8]Consolidated Electors Brief, page 19.
[9]Ibid. at 24.
[10]Ibid. at 29.

The presidential electors also argue that the Founders plainly anticipated that electors would be free agents who would exercise independent
choice. While some Framers supported direct election of the President,
they were concerned about the practical reality of nationwide commu-
nication in 1787, and thus created an intermediate body. As Alexander
Hamilton explained in *Federalist* 68, states would appoint electors who
would be the "most likely to possess the information and discernment
requisite" to casting a vote for president and thus be the "most capable
of analyzing [presidential] qualities."[11] The Electoral College, Hamilton
explained, set forth "circumstances favorable to deliberation," and the
electors argue that this deliberation is evidence that they were to exercise
independent judgment.[12]

The electors claim that the Twelfth Amendment did not alter the
independence of electors contemplated by the Constitution. It fixed
a flaw in the original design by requiring electors to vote separately
for president and vice president, but "left elector freedom untouched."
Indeed, even though 40% of the electors in the 1796 presidential election voted contrary to expectation, the drafters of the Amendment "did
not even consider a rule to bind electors to the will of their appointing
Legislature."[13]

The electors contend that an "early and unbroken history of anoma-
lous voting by presidential electors," shows that electors may not be
directed by a state. Rather, "Congress has long recognized the right of
electors to vote contrary to their pledge or expectation."[14] Specifically,
across the nation's history, Congress has counted more than 180 anoma-
lous electoral votes for either President or Vice President, and no such
votes have ever been rejected. Even if our current political culture views
electors as mere delegates, the electors argue that the Constitution may
not be amended by custom or public expectation and no source of law
has transformed the power *to appoint* into the power to control how an
elector *votes*.

---

[11]Ibid. at 19.
[12]Ibid. at 37.
[13]Ibid. at 36.
[14]Ibid. at 16, 46.

The states dispute the electors' interpretation of constitutional text and history. They argue that, because the Constitution authorizes states to "appoint" electors "in such Manner as the Legislature thereof may direct," and because the default rule is that the power to appoint includes the power to remove, the appointment power necessarily includes the right to control a state's electors. The electors' arguments regarding the meaning of the terms "electors," "appoint," "vote," and "ballot," are belied by other contemporary definitions and by long-standing historical practice: since the first presidential election, electors have been chosen based on their pledge to support particular candidates, and states have removed and replaced electors who violated the conditions of their appointment.

In addition, the states argue that the Framers spent very little time discussing the electors during the Constitutional Convention and that Hamilton's view that electors would exercise discretion was contradicted by other Framers who stated that the mode of electing the president depended ultimately on the people. In all events, the states argue that the Electoral College was significantly revised by the Twelfth Amendment. By the time the Amendment was adopted, its Framers had "a clear shared understanding that 'electors' were expected to follow the will of the people."[15]

Further, the states' undoubted "power to establish requirements for state elections, including the selection of presidential electors" would be meaningless without the ability to enforce those requirements.[16] States would be unable to remove electors who failed to meet age or residency requirements as well as those who took a bribe or skipped the electors' meeting. That Congress may have counted faithless ballots in the past, when states did not have faithless elector laws, says little about the ability of states to enforce statutory requirements. Indeed, in 2016, Congress counted two ballots from electors whom the state had chosen to replace as faithless electors.

Another foundation of the states' claim of authority is the constitutional principle of *federalism*. Justice Anthony Kennedy described the

---

[15]Washington Brief at 25–26.
[16]Colorado Brief at 20.

principle as the constitutional structure whereby the Framers "split the atom of sovereignty," granting certain limited powers to the federal government and reserving the remainder for the various state governments.[17] The states claim that the "Tenth Amendment's reservation of residual state power likewise corroborates the States' plenary authority over their appointed electors."[18]

The states argue that all of the relevant actors—states, electors, Congress, the public, and the Supreme Court—have long understood that the electors' role is "to register the will of the" state.[19] Less than "one percent [of electors] have ever been faithless" and most states have stopped listing electors' names on the ballot "because their identities are irrelevant."[20] The states conclude that for the Court to find that electors have discretion would "upend long-settled expectations and undermine Americans' confidence that their votes have any meaning."[21]

The Unanimous Ruling

In an opinion written by Justice Elena Kagan, the full Supreme Court sided with the states, holding that the power to appoint electors "in such Manner as the Legislature thereof may direct," gives the States "far-reaching authority over presidential electors." The power to appoint includes the power to condition such appointment. Thus, a State can require an elector to live in the State, or pledge to cast his ballot for his party's presidential nominee. And so long as nothing else in the Constitution poses an obstacle, a State "can demand that the elector actually live up to his pledge, on pain of penalty."[22]

Justice Kagan noted that the Framers could have done it differently, and indeed, the Constitutions of Maryland and Kentucky expressly vested discretion on electors. But no similar language made it into

---

[17] *U.S. Term Limits, Inc. v. Thornton*, 514 U.S. 779 (1995) at 838 (Kennedy concurrence).
[18] Colorado Brief, page 9.
[19] Ibid. at 20.
[20] Washington Brief, page 21.
[21] Ibid.
[22] All quotes from *Chiafalo* decision, pages 9-10.

the Constitution. The Court found the electors' reliance on the terms "elector," "vote," and "ballot" insufficient to command elector discretion. As for the views of Alexander Hamilton and John Jay expressed in the *Federalist Papers*, even if other Framers shared these views they did not commit those thoughts about elector discretion to the printed page.

Further, the Court held that "long settled and established practice" may have "great weight in a proper interpretation of constitutional provisions." Our "whole experience as a nation" establishes that electors "have only rarely exercised discretion." From the beginning, states sent electors to vote for predetermined candidates. The Twelfth Amendment acknowledged and facilitated the Electoral College's emergence as a non-discretionary mechanism for party-line voting. Throughout the nineteenth century, courts and commentators recognized the "electors as merely acting on other people's preferences."[23] Unsurprisingly, state election law evolved to ensure that a State's electors would vote the same way as its citizens.

In short, the Court found that the argument for elector discretion has "neither text nor history on its side."[24] Rather, Article II and the Twelfth Amendment both give the States broad power over electors, and for more than 200 years, states have tied electors to the presidential choices of others. As a result, the States might enforce statutory penalties against faithless electors.

Justice Thomas concurred only in the result. In his view, the majority's reliance on Article II was misplaced because the Constitution "does not speak to States' power to require Presidential electors to vote for the candidates chosen by the people."[25] Joined by Justice Gorsuch, Thomas grounded his opinion in the principle of federalism, explaining that, "[w]here the Constitution is silent about the exercise of a particular power... the power is 'either delegated to the state government or retained by the people.'"[26] As a result, the States hold the authority

---

[23]Ibid. at 15–16.
[24]Ibid. at 17.
[25] *Chiafalo* Thomas concurrence, page 9.
[26]Ibid., page 11, quoting his dissent in *US Term Limits v. Thornton* (1995).

to regulate electors (to the extent not specifically prohibited by the Constitution).

Looking Ahead

As of July 6, 2020—the day *Chiafalo* was decided—thirty-three states and the District of Columbia had laws mandating that presidential electors cast ballots for the candidate chosen by the voters of their state. In sixteen of those States and in the District of Columbia, however, there is no legal mechanism to enforce this mandate.[27] *Chiafalo* makes clear a state has the constitutional authority (but not the necessity) to adopt and enforce a statute mandating that presidential electors cast ballots for the candidate chosen by the voters of their state. Whether more states will do so after the *Chiafalo* ruling remains to be seen.

In 2010, the Uniform Law Commission drafted the Faithful Presidential Electors Act as a model for states. The legislation requires presidential electors to take a state-administered pledge of faithfulness, cancels any faithless vote, and replaces any faithless elector. At the time of the Court's decision in *Chiafalo*, six states had adopted this model legislation.[28] There will likely be a push in the years ahead for states to adopt either this model legislation or other legislative initiatives which bind and penalize electors.

A related political movement has also developed in recent years: the National Popular Vote Interstate Compact. The NPVIC would be an agreement among the states that collectively control a majority of Electoral College votes to mandate that their state's presidential electors vote for the candidate who wins the national popular vote. According to National Popular Vote Inc.—an organization advocating for the adoption of the National Popular Vote bill state by state—sixteen states controlling 196 electoral votes have enacted the legislation, which only goes into effect if it is adopted by enough states to control a majority (270) of the electoral votes.

---

[27]Fair Vote. https://infogram.com/states-laws-binding-electors-1g9vp1ywyrxlp4y.
[28]www.uniformlaws.org.

The Supreme Court did not address the constitutionality of the NPVIC, but *Chiafalo* is potentially relevant to the ongoing movement for a national popular vote. As the majority opinion noted, since the nineteenth century, states have consistently sought to ensure that presidential electors vote for the candidate chosen by *their* state's electorate. "Washington law, penalizing a pledge's breach," the Court writes, "is only another in the same vein. It reflects a tradition more than two centuries old. In that practice, electors are not free agents; they are to vote for the candidate whom the State's voters have chosen."[29]

A question now opened by *Chiafalo* is what textual, historical, or structural principles limit the constitutional discretion of a state to "appoint, in such Manner as the Legislature thereof may direct, a Number of Electors."[30] If the long-established practice of the Electoral College is to represent the citizens of states *as* states, is there a constitutional reason why a state legislature may not alter that long-standing practice to award the state's electoral votes to the reflect the will of the majority of voters of the nation? For now, this much is clear: a state may bind its presidential electors to the will of the state's electorate through legal mechanisms that penalize or cancel a faithless vote in the Electoral College.

---

[29] *Chiafalo* decision, page 16.
[30] U.S. Constitution, Art. II., Sec. 1, Cl. 2

4

Department of Homeland Security v. University of California on DACA

John C. Eastman

On June 18, 2020, the Supreme Court rejected the Trump administration's efforts to rescind the Deferred Action for Childhood Arrivals
(DACA) program that suspends deportation of nearly 900,000 residents
who arrived in the United States illegally as children or young adults.[1]
The program, which was adopted as an asserted exercise in prosecutorial
discretion that could be revoked at any time, provided renewable deferments from deportation for two years at a time, but did not provide
permanent status. It also provided a host of other benefits for those who
were granted "deferred action," such as work authorization, Social Security, and Medicare. Since its inception, the program has been criticized as
an unconstitutional exercise of presidential power, without congressional
approval of its dramatic shift in immigration policy.

---

[1] The total number of possible recipients is approximately 1.7 million.

J. C. Eastman (✉)
Center for Constitutional Jurisprudence,
Claremont Institute, Upland, CA, USA

© The Author(s) 2021
M. Marietta (ed.), *SCOTUS 2020*,
https://doi.org/10.1007/978-3-030-53851-4_4

Surprisingly, the ruling in *Department of Homeland Security v. Regents of the University of California* does not address the legality of the DACA program; instead, it focuses on the *process* by which the Trump administration attempted to rescind it. In halting, perhaps only temporarily, the rescission of DACA on the grounds that it violates the process requirements of the Administrative Procedure Act, the Court breaks new ground. The ruling requires a presidential administration to put forth arguments the Court considers to be complete, candid, and considering all the relevant factors before shifting course from a prior administration's policies or risk the actions of executive agencies being struck down.

Background

The DACA program was created through the actions of an executive agency rather than congressional law, when on June 15, 2012, President Barack Obama's Secretary of Homeland Security, Janet Napolitano, issued the DACA memo ostensibly as an exercise in prosecutorial discretion over which immigrants the administration would or would not deport. This was followed in 2014 by the creation of DAPA, a second program applying the same deferments to the *parents* of DACA recipients, an additional 3–4 million people. DAPA was enjoined by a federal court in Texas for likely procedural violations of the Administrative Procedure Act, a decision that was affirmed by the Fifth Circuit on both procedural and substantive grounds.[2] The injunction against DAPA was upheld by a divided Court (4-4) after the passing of Justice Antonin Scalia.[3] DACA remained in place until rescinded by the Trump administration in a memorandum by Acting Secretary Elaine Duke, with a second memorandum further justifying the decision issued by her successor, Secretary Kirstjen Nielsen.

Several plaintiffs, led by the University of California—whose President, Janet Napolitano, issued the original DACA memo while DHS

---

[2] *Texas v. United States*, 86 F.Supp.3d 591 (S.D. Tex. 2015) and *Texas v. United States*, 809 F.3d 134 (5th Cir. 2015).

[3] See *US v. Texas* (2016), which reads in its entirety, "The judgment is affirmed by an equally divided Court."

Secretary under the Obama administration—brought a petition for an injunction blocking the rescission. The Ninth Circuit Court of Appeals affirmed the nationwide injunction and the Supreme Court agreed to hear the case in June of 2019, issuing its ruling twelve months later in June of 2020.

The Constitutional and Procedural Flaws with the DACA Program

The 2012 DACA program (and its 2014 cousin, DAPA) had significant constitutional as well as procedural problems.

DACA was an unconstitutional suspension of the law. Although Napolitano's memo was couched repeatedly in terms of "case by case prosecutorial discretion," it actually amounted to a wholesale suspension of the law for an entire category of people who were illegally present in the United States. For anyone meeting the criteria set out in the memo—approximately 1.7 million people—the Administration would not undertake removal proceedings.

The notion that this memo allowed for a true individualized determination, rather than a categorical suspension of the law, is simply not credible. There is nothing in the memo to suggest that immigration officials could do anything other than defer deportation proceedings against those meeting the defined eligibility criteria. By repeatedly invoking the phrase, "on a case by case basis," however, Secretary Napolitano seemed to recognize the long-standing requirement that prosecutorial discretion cannot be exercised categorically without crossing the line into unconstitutional suspension of the law, violating the President's constitutional obligation to "take care that the laws be faithfully executed."[4] And yet, the DACA memo did just that.

---

[4] See, e.g., *Heckler v. Cheney*, 470 U.S. at 832–833 no. 4 (1985) finding that judicial review is appropriate when an agency has adopted a general policy that is an "abdication of its statutory responsibilities." The opinion put out by the Office of Legal Counsel at the Department of Justice to defend the 2014 DAPA program recognized this: "[T]he Executive Branch ordinarily cannot ... consciously and expressly adopt a general policy that is so extreme as to amount to an abdication of its statutory responsibilities." Karl R. Thompson, Office of Legal Counsel, "The Department of Homeland Security's Authority to Prioritize Removal of Certain Aliens

DACA's grant of "lawful presence" and financial benefits was without statutory or constitutional authority. Even if Secretary Napolitano's DACA directive could properly be viewed as an exercise of prosecutorial discretion, the DACA program went a significant step further, as Chief Justice Roberts recognized in his opinion for the Court.[5] When Napolitano ordered the Immigration Service to "accept applications to determine whether these individuals qualify for work authorization during this period of deferred action," she turned a questionable exercise of prosecutorial discretion into an illegal grant of benefits.[6] This is contrary to the Constitution's Article I, Section 8 assignment of authority over immigration and naturalization to Congress, as well as Article I, Section 9's requirement that no money be drawn from the treasury "but in consequence of appropriations made by law."

The notion that prosecutorial discretion could be used not just to decline to prosecute or deport, but also to confer a lawful presence, work authorization, and other benefits as well, required a distortion of the doctrine of prosecutorial discretion beyond recognition. The memo cited no legal authority for this extraordinary claim, and it was directly contradicted by legal advice given by the INS's general counsel during the Clinton Administration.[7] Simply put, only the Congress has the constitutional authority for such a change in immigration policy, not the President at his own discretion.

DACA was implemented without going through the notice and comment rulemaking process required by the Administrative Procedure Act. Finally,

---

Unlawfully Present in the United States and to Defer Removal of Others" (19 November 2014), page 7.

[5]*DHS* decision, pages 11–12.

[6]As the US Customs and Immigration Service explained on its website, "An individual who has received deferred action… is therefore considered by DHS to be *lawfully present* during the period of deferred action is in effect" (emphasis added). Hence hundreds of thousands of DACA applicants were deemed eligible for work authorization and other benefits available only to those who are lawfully present in the United States.

[7]See Bo Cooper, General Counsel, "INS Exercise of Prosecutorial Discretion" (11 July 2000) at 4, available at https://tinyurl.com/CooperMemo ("The doctrine of prosecutorial discretion applies to enforcement decisions, not benefit decisions. For example, a decision to charge, or not to charge, an alien with a ground of deportability is clearly a prosecutorial enforcement decision. By contrast, the grant of an immigration benefit, such as naturalization or adjustment of status, is a benefit decision that is not a subject for prosecutorial discretion.")

DACA was also procedurally flawed. It amounted to a major policy change that was required to, but did not, go through the notice and comment rulemaking process of the Administrative Procedure Act.[8] Although the subsequent 4-4 ruling of the Supreme Court in *U.S. v. Texas* in 2016 addressed only the DAPA program, the DACA program stands (or falls) on the same constitutional, statutory, and procedural grounds.

The Supreme Court's DACA Ruling

In most cases before the Court, one would expect the constitutional, statutory, and procedural infirmities of an agency's action to frame the discussion over the validity of the decision to rescind it. An unconstitutional action instituted by one administration can surely be removed by another. Instead the Court focused on an entirely different approach, creating a more stringent standard of review under the Administrative Procedure Act.[9]

Perhaps the key to understanding the Court's ruling occurred in the oral arguments during an exchange between Justice Brett Kavanaugh and the advocate for the DACA recipients (Ted Olson, former US Solicitor General).[10]

Justice Kavanaugh: Do you agree that the executive has the legal authority to rescind DACA?
Mr. Olson: Yes.
Justice Kavanaugh: Okay. So the question then comes down to the explanation.

---

[8] Designed to provide some measure of political accountability by unelected officials in executive agencies, the APA requires agencies to publish a *notice* of their intended new policies and rules in order to give the public an opportunity to *comment* on them before the policies can be put into effect.

[9] See Thomas dissent: "the majority simply opts to excise the 'unlawful policy' aspect from its discussion," page 23.

[10] *DHS* oral arguments transcript, 12 November 2019, page 61.

Chief Justice Roberts affirmed this view in the Court's decision: "The dispute before the Court is not whether DHS may rescind DACA. All parties agree that it may. The dispute is instead primarily about the procedure the agency followed in doing so."[11] Both sides agreed that the administration had the power to repeal the program, *if they had done it right*; the only question was whether the administration had adequately and fully explained the reasons for its decision as required by the APA. This more stringent standard of review employed by the Court has two parts:

The Court must consider only the original justifications offered by the administration. Roberts explains that "it is a foundational principle of administrative law that judicial review of agency action is limited to the grounds the agency invoked when it took the action."[12] For this reason, the Court only considered the first memorandum, issued by Acting Secretary Duke in 2017 at the time of the initial rescission of DACA, but not the subsequent memorandum providing further justification issued by Secretary Nielsen nine months later. In Roberts' view, later considerations "can be viewed only as impermissible post hoc rationalizations and thus are not properly before" the Court.[13] He concluded that "the basic rule here is clear: An agency must defend its actions based on the reasons it gave when it acted."[14] The administration must explain adequately *the first time*, not in later, supplemental memoranda after being challenged.

Justice Kavanaugh's dissent disputes this rule when applied to subsequent actors within the same administration. The first memorandum was issued by one DHS Secretary, and the second by another, offering her own justification. In Kavanaugh's view, just as one official is not bound by the decision of their predecessor, neither are they bound by those earlier justifications, but may offer different or additional ones. The traditional rule disallowing post hoc justifications for agency action had previously been applied in the context of positions advanced by an

---

[11] *DHS* decision, page 9.

[12] Ibid. at 13.

[13] Ibid. at 15. The first memo "makes no mention of a preference for legislative fixes, the superiority of case-by-case decisionmaking, the importance of sending a message of robust enforcement, or any other policy consideration."

[14] Ibid. at 17.

agency's lawyers *in litigation*.[15] Roberts' extension of the post hoc rule to supplemental justifications offered by the agency itself therefore broke new ground, perhaps driven by Roberts' apparent suspicion that Trump and his administration may not have been fully candid in their explanation of the policy change, the same suspicion that appears to have been driving Roberts' decision a year earlier when he cast the deciding vote to block the Trump Administration from restoring a citizenship question to the Census.[16]

The Trump administration failed to acknowledge the reliance interests of the DACA recipients as a conspicuous fact. The second core claim at the heart of the Court's ruling is that the administration did not consider the interests of the DACA recipients or discuss the full set of negative ramifications for the individuals and families involved. The legal term for the expectations set up by laws or administrative rules is *reliance interests.* In the Court's view, DHS "was required to assess whether there were reliance interests, determine whether they were significant, and weigh any such interests against competing policy concerns."[17] In that sense, the Secretary of DHS "failed to consider... important aspects of the problem before her," and "the agency failed to consider the conspicuous issues of whether to retain forbearance and what if anything to do about the hardship to DACA recipients."[18] The Court concluded that "Acting Secretary Duke should have considered those matters but did not. That failure was arbitrary and capricious in violation of the APA."[19]

The government argued that Acting Secretary Duke did not need to consider reliance interests because the DACA program itself made clear that no reliance interests were created. The program was, the government argued, "a temporary, discretionary policy; was granted in two-year increments; and created no lawful status or substantive rights."[20] The

---

[15] "I am aware of no case from this Court, and this Court today cites none, that has employed the post hoc justification doctrine to exclude an agency's official explanation of an agency rule." Kavanaugh dissent, page 6.

[16] *Department of Commerce v. New York* (2019).

[17] *DHS* decision, page 26.

[18] Ibid. at 18, 29.

[19] Ibid. at 26. Secretary Nielson *did* consider reliance interests, but because that was in the subsequent memo it did not count according to the first part of the Court's holding.

[20] *DHS* Reply Brief, page 17.

government asserted that under these conditions, "the DACA policy could not engender any legally cognizable reliance interests."[21]

Another way of phrasing the Court's ruling rejecting DHS's argument is that a federal agency is required to consider all of the relevant facts (as judged by the Court), even if the agency itself does not believe them to be relevant. But how would the government actors know which facts have to be considered? Which are "conspicuous"? What is the standard for a fact being important enough that it has to be considered, officially and on paper, or risk the Court ruling the omission arbitrary and capricious? · Is there a standard for recognizing "conspicuous facts" that is itself not arbitrary and capricious? The Court does not say.

In his dissent, Justice Clarence Thomas (joined by Samuel Alito and Neil Gorsuch) described the decision as "mystifying."[22] His core argument is that DACA was unlawful from the outset, so rescinding it could not be unlawful.[23] Regarding the conspicuous nature of the reliance interests involved, he pointed out that the DACA memorandum explicitly states that the program "confers no substantive right or immigration status" because "only the Congress, acting through its legislative authority, can confer these rights."[24] Thomas noted that the DAPA memorandum in 2014 made the same assertions. He concluded that "as a general matter, deferred action creates no rights—it exists at the Government's discretion and can be revoked at any time."[25] Hence "nothing in the APA suggests that DHS was required to spill any ink justifying the rescission of an invalid legislative rule."[26] If the original DACA memorandum and DHS in legal proceedings asserted that no

---

[21] *DHS* decision, page 26.

[22] Thomas dissent, page 2.

[23] "DHS had no authority to create DACA, and the unlawfulness of that program is a sufficient justification for its rescission… In implementing DACA, DHS under the Obama administration arrogated to itself power it was not given by Congress. Thus, every action taken by DHS under DACA is the unlawful exercise of power." Ibid. at 15, 16.

[24] Ibid. at 5. The DACA memo itself expressly stated that it "confers no substantive right, immigration status or pathway to citizenship," and the DACA application form itself advised applicants that "Deferred action does not confer lawful status upon an individual" and that "a decision on deferred action is wholly within the discretion of DHS."

[25] Ibid. at 23.

[26] Ibid. at 19.

reliance interests were created, it was reasonable to believe that those facts were not "conspicuous" and hence could not be mandatory for DHS to consider.

In sum, the DACA decision announces a rule that a presidential administration must, when implementing a policy change, be fully comprehensive in its justifications, the first time, in the judgment of the Court. This is a new and radical understanding of the requirements of the Administrative Procedure Act. The legal argument—and now Supreme Court doctrine—that failing to explain all the reasons for a policy change is grounds for striking down government action may have tremendous ramifications.[27] Essentially the Court has announced that it is the new arbiter of candor in our polarized politics.

The End Result

Finally, we should not conclude our analysis of the Court's DACA decision without mentioning the partisan and electoral ramifications. Given the popularity of the DACA program (at least, according to polls) Democrat partisans could easily suspect that Chief Justice Roberts joined with the four liberal Justices in this 5-4 ruling in order to forestall a rescission of the program taking effect before the November presidential election.[28] Justice Thomas' statement in dissent that the "decision must be recognized for what it is: an effort to avoid a politically controversial but legally correct decision" might be read as lending some credibility to such a suspicion.[29] Or it could be read, alternatively, as lending credence to a counter suspicion on the Republican side of the partisan divide,

---

[27]For a discussion of similar reasoning in the census citizenship ruling in 2019, in which Roberts called out the administration for "pretext" and "contrived" arguments when the "evidence tells a story that does not match the explanation," see Chapter 3 in *SCOTUS 2019*, "*Department of Commerce v. New York* on the Census Citizenship Question" by Brett Curry. Roberts' assertion in the census case met with deep disdain from Justice Thomas, who wrote: "For the first time ever, the court invalidates an agency action solely because it questions the sincerity of the agency's otherwise adequate rationale" (Thomas dissent, page 1).

[28]See Chantal De Silva, "74 Percent of Americans Support Legal Status for DACA Dreamers, Poll Finds," *Newsweek* (18 June 2020); Brett Samuels, "Poll: Most Americans Support DACA," *The Hill* (14 January 2018).

[29]Thomas dissent, pages 2–3.

that a majority of the Court simply disagrees with the policy judgment made by the current President and hopes that by delaying the decision until past the 2020 election the time available for rescinding DACA will expire (even while that same Court majority acknowledged that the President does have the authority to rescind an agency action if the proper procedure is followed).

But whatever the motive behind the Court's decision, the current Acting Secretary of the Department of Homeland Security is not barred by the decision from rescinding the DACA program. He simply needs to go through a few additional APA hoops to do so. Whether the clock will run out on the current administration's term in office before than can be accomplished remains to be seen. Under normal timetables that process could not be completed before November. But the APA itself allows for an expedited adoption of new rules "for good cause found."[30] Particularly in light of Justice Thomas' persuasive argument in dissent that DACA was itself "unlawful and would force DHS to continue acting unlawfully if it carried the program forward"—a conclusion that the majority did not dispute—the grounds for expedited adoption of a rule rescinding DACA are at least as solid as past uses of the provision. Should the Department of Homeland Security readopt a rescission rule on an expedited basis, there would undoubtedly be a political firestorm of opposition by pro-DACA partisans. But failure to act would likely cause a political firestorm from the other side as well. In other words, by ignoring DACA's illegality and focusing on a novel theory of procedural adequacy and candor, the Court has all but guaranteed a tempestuous fight over the issue going into an election season already overflowing with tempestuous issues.

---

[30] 5 U.S.C. § 553(d)(3). This process was employed by the Obama administration when it adopted the contraceptive mandate for insurance plans under the Affordable Care Act without going through the required notice and comment rulemaking process and by waiving the 30–day minimum effective date for new rules.

5

Espinoza, Lady of Guadalupe, and *Little Sisters of the Poor* on Religious Liberty

Kevin Pybas

In the last week of its 2019–2020 term the Supreme Court resolved three cases in favor of religious liberty claims. Different facts and legal foundations caution against sweeping generalizations about what the cases tell us about the current state of play in the Court's religious liberty jurisprudence. Still, they indicate a majority of Justices supporting the equal treatment of religious institutions in public benefit programs, and an even stronger majority willing to exempt religious institutions from some of the legislative burdens imposed by the contemporary regulatory state.

In the case with perhaps the most far-reaching consequences, which helps explain the 5-4 vote and the seven different written opinions, the Court held in *Espinoza v. Montana Department of Revenue* that the Free Exercise Clause of the First Amendment mandates that government benefit programs must treat religious service providers equal to secular counterparts. In a 7-2 decision, the Court ruled in *Our Lady of Guadalupe School v. Morrissey-Berru* that both the Establishment

K. Pybas (✉)
Missouri State University, Springfield, MO, USA

© The Author(s) 2021
M. Marietta (ed.), *SCOTUS 2020*,
https://doi.org/10.1007/978-3-030-53851-4_5

and Free Exercise Clauses prohibit courts from adjudicating employment discrimination claims against religious schools brought by teachers who fit within the "ministerial exception" because their responsibilities include instilling the school's faith. In the most factually complicated of the cases, by a 7-2 vote the Court ruled in *Little Sisters of the Poor Saints Peter and Paul Home v. Pennsylvania* that an administrative rule exempting religious employers who object to including contraception in their insurance plans was lawfully issued. This is unlikely the final word on this long-standing dispute, as other administrative issues that could affect the outcome continue to lurk.

Espinoza v. Montana Department of Revenue

Espinoza follows from the Court's decision in 2017 in *Trinity Lutheran*, which held that the exclusion of a church from a public benefit—in this case the resurfacing of daycare playgrounds—solely because of its status as a church violated the Free Exercise Clause.[1] Here the issue was a provision in the Montana constitution prohibiting the state from making "any direct or indirect appropriation or payment … for any sectarian purpose or to aid any church [or] school … controlled in whole or in part by any church [or] denomination." The Montana Supreme Court had ruled that the no-aid provision prohibited scholarships funded by a state tax-credit plan from being used in religious schools. The law permitted scholarships to be used in private nonreligious and religious schools on an equal basis, but the state court struck the entire program because there was no means within it to prevent scholarship money from being distributed to the religious schools.

Espinoza illustrates the tension in free exercise and antiestablishment values. Both the Establishment and Free Exercise Clauses limit government, but in different ways. The Establishment Clause prevents government from promoting, favoring, or involving itself with religion, while the Free Exercise Clause prohibits government from interfering with religious practices and generally requires religion to be treated equal

---

[1] *Trinity Lutheran Church of Columbia, Inc. v. Comer*, 528 U.S. __ (2017).

to nonreligion. For about forty years the Court has ruled that the Establishment Clause is not violated when public funds are used in religious schools upon the free choice of aid recipients. Hence the tax-credit program raises no Establishment Clause issue. Instead, the issue concerns the "play in the joints" between the two clauses. Given that the scholarships are *permitted* by the Establishment Clause, are they also *required* by the Free Exercise Clause? Put otherwise, does Montana's effort to separate itself from religion (more than is required by the Establishment Cause), result in treating religion worse than nonreligion and hence violate the Free Exercise Clause?[2]

Chief Justice Robert's opinion for the Court, joined by Justices Thomas, Alito, Gorsuch, and Kavanaugh, held that the no-aid provision of the Montana constitution "discriminates based on religious status," because it denies a public benefit to religious schools simply because they are religious. Consequently, to pass Free Exercise Clause scrutiny, the state had to show that the provision furthered a compelling state interest that could not be achieved in a less discriminatory way. The Montana Department of Revenue defended the no-aid provision on the grounds that it (1) promotes the state's preference for greater separation between government and religion than is required by the Establishment Clause, (2) furthers the religious liberty of taxpayers who object to public money being used in religious schools, as well as the liberty of religious schools by keeping government out of their business, and (3) protects public schools by keeping education money from private schools. The Court held that these interests are not compelling enough to override the protections of the Free Exercise Clause. This is especially the case because the provision did not prohibit tax dollars from being used in nonreligious private schools, and hence the third claim that it protected the funding of public education is clearly not compelling.

Justice Thomas concurred (joined by Justice Gorsuch), arguing as he long has that the Court's Establishment Clause jurisprudence needs to be

---

[2]For further discussion of the meaning and requirements of the dual Religion Clauses, see *SCOTUS 2018* Chapter 6 on "*Masterpiece Cakeshop* on Gay Rights Versus Religious Liberty," by Stephen Engel, and *SCOTUS 2019* Chapter 2 on "*American Legion v. American Humanist* on Religious Monuments Under the First Amendment," by Ronald Kahn and Gerard D'Emilio.

reworked because it impedes free exercise rights. Justice Alito's concurrence lays out the nineteenth-century anti-Catholic origin of the no-aid clause in the Montana constitution (and in many other state constitutions) and argues that its readoption in 1972 did not remove the original taint of religious bigotry, which is an additional reason for its unconstitutionality.

In his dissent, Justice Breyer (joined in part by Justice Kagan), argues that the no-aid provision permissibly prohibits public funds from being used in religious schools. Breyer and Kagan were in the 7-2 majority in *Trinity Lutheran* insisting that religious institutions be included in government programs, but here Justice Breyer argues that the tax-credit program funds "the inculcation of religious truths," which is different than denying a church the opportunity to compete for a grant to obtain playground resurfacing material as in *Trinity Lutheran*. Justice Breyer argues that *Locke v. Davey* is the controlling precedent, that although the Establishment Clause permits a state to include religious schools in a neutral tax-credit program, the Free Exercise Clause does not mandate that the state include them.[3]

Justice Ginsburg's dissent, joined by Justice Kagan, argues that the case involves no religious discrimination because the Montana Supreme Court invalidated the entire scholarship program, so all private schools were treated equally. Justice Sotomayor makes the same point in her dissent and criticizes the majority for taking up the free exercise claim when it had not been adjudicated by the Montana Supreme Court.

Our Lady of Guadalupe School v. Morrissey-Berru

The ruling in *Lady of Guadalupe* rests on the "ministerial exception," a doctrine grounded in both the Establishment and Free Exercise Clauses, protecting the autonomy of religious institutions to select or replace staff who are central to the promulgation of their faith, free of government regulation. Although the principle had been recognized by lower

---

[3]540 U.S. 712 (2004).

courts for some time, recognition by the Court did not come until 2012 in *Hosanna-Tabor Evangelical Lutheran Church v. EEOC*, which was a unanimous decision.[4] *Lady of Guadalupe* represents the Court's first application of its *Hosanna-Tabor* analysis.

At issue was whether federal antidiscrimination claims made by teachers against two Catholic elementary schools could be adjudicated. (*Lady of Guadalupe* was combined with *St. James School v. Biel*). According to the schools, the teachers were dismissed because of poor classroom performance. However, one argued her contract was not renewed because the school wanted to replace her with someone younger, and the other contended she was let go because she had asked for a medical leave of absence. Those claims would justify a legal cause of action unless the schools were exempt from those employment regulations. The schools insisted that because the teachers had important roles in teaching Catholicism to students, the decisions to dismiss them fell within the ministerial exception. Both schools prevailed on summary judgment in district court but both were reversed by panels of the US Court of Appeals for the Ninth Circuit.

The Supreme Court held that both panels of the Ninth Circuit "misunderstood" *Hosanna-Tabor*. In that case a unanimous Court ruled that a teacher's discrimination claim could not be adjudicated because of her role in promulgating the faith of the school. The Court said "all the circumstances" of the employee's job are to be considered, and concluded the exception applied because the teacher (1) had the title of minister, (2) had substantial religious training, (3) held herself out as a minister of the church that operated the school, and (4) had a significant role in inculcating the church's faith in students.

Justice Alito wrote for the Court in *Lady of Guadalupe*, concluding that the Ninth Circuit panels treated the four factors as "checklist items to be assessed and weighed against each other." Specifically, the Courts of Appeal emphasized that the teachers did not have ministerial titles and that they had less formal religious education than the teacher in *Hosanna-Tabor*. This inflexible checklist approach, the Court answered,

---

[4]565 U.S. 171 (2012).

"distorted" the extent of the teachers' involvement in the spiritual development of their students. This led the Ninth Circuit to substitute their beliefs about proper credentials for teaching religion for the judgment of the schools. *Lady of Guadalupe* thus makes no new law. It corrects a misapplication of *Hosanna-Tabor* and reasserts that in deciding the applicability of the ministerial exception, "all relevant circumstances" regarding the teacher's role are to be considered.[5]

Justice Thomas concurred, joined by Justice Gorsuch, arguing that whether a position qualifies as ministerial or not is a theological question and thus is one the Free Exercise and Establishment Clauses prohibit courts from answering. Consequently, courts must accept a religious organization's "good faith" designation that a position is ministerial. *Hosanna-Tabor* was a unanimous decision but Justice Sotomayor, joined by Justice Ginsburg, dissented here. She accused the majority of being overly deferential to the schools' claims that the teachers had important religious roles, which potentially leaves many religious school employees without recourse for workplace discrimination. The limit of the ministerial exception, beyond teachers to coaches, counselors, or cooks remains unclear.

Little Sisters of the Poor Saints Peter and Paul Home v. Pennsylvania

Little Sisters represents the latest, though possibly not the last, wrangling over implementation of the Patient Protection and Affordable Care Act of 2010 (the ACA, otherwise known as Obamacare). At issue in *Little Sisters* (consolidated with *Trump v. Pennsylvania*) was the legality of 2017 federal administrative rules exempting certain employers with religious and moral objections from compliance with the contraception mandate under the ACA. The States of Pennsylvania and New Jersey argued that federal departments issuing the exemptions lacked statutory authority to do so and that they failed to follow proper administrative procedures when promulgating the exemptions.

---

[5] *Lady of Guadalupe* decision, pages 22, 23.

The ACA requires employers subject to the law to provide "preventative care and screenings" in their insurance plans for female employees. But Congress left it to the Health Resources and Services Administration to specify the exact care and screening to be provided. In 2011 the agency mandated that coverage had to include all contraceptives and sterilization methods approved by the Food and Drug Administration. The mandate was to take effect in August 2012, but before it did the Department of Health and Human Services exempted certain religious employers, primarily churches, from the contraception mandate. Because of complaints from religious nonprofits not covered by the initial exemption, an additional religious exemption was issued in 2013. This regulation required covered religious organizations to "self-certify" that they were eligible for the exemption. They had to provide the self-certification form to their health insurance provider, which would then exclude contraception care from the organization's health insurance plan, but pay for the cost of those female employees to acquire the services.[6]

When the exemption became effective in 2013, lawsuits were filed across the nation challenging the adequacy of it, including one by Little Sisters of the Poor, an international order of Roman Catholic nuns who serve the elderly poor. Little Sisters objected that self-certification made it complicit in providing, or appearing to provide, contraception, and thus violated their religious beliefs in violation of the federal Religious Freedom Restoration Act of 1993 (RFRA). According to RFRA, federal laws substantially burdening religion must serve a compelling governmental interest and must be crafted to further that interest in the least burdensome way.[7] Lower federal courts agreed with the Departments' argument that self-certification did not substantially burden the exercise of religion, and thus did not violate RFRA. The Court took the case and several similar ones but ultimately remanded them back to lower

---

[6]Hence the Little Sisters would not be paying for contraception, and the female employees would not be denied them, with the insurance company covering the costs. In the view of the Little Sisters, one of them sending a form telling the company to arrange for contraception and simply shifting the expense was taking actions complicit in providing those services.

[7]RFRA was Congress' response to a 1990 Supreme Court decision (*Employment Division v. Smith*, 494 U.S. 872) which made it more difficult to establishment a Free Exercise Clause violation. RFRA imposes on federal laws a higher standard than the Court says is necessary under the Free Exercise Clause.

courts to allow the parties to try to reach an acceptable accommodation. In doing so, the Court instructed the government to both "accommodate the [organizations'] religious exercise [and] ensure that women covered by [their] health plans receive full and equal coverage, including contraceptive care."[8] Despite the Court's charge, in 2016 the Departments concluded that no accommodation was possible and reasserted their position that self-certification did not substantially burden religious exercise or, if it did, no less burdensome means existed for achieving the government's compelling interest in women's healthcare.

Enter the Trump Administration in 2017, which renewed efforts to accommodate the religious institutions and created the two rules at issue here. Notably, the Departments now agreed with Little Sisters that the self-certification process violated RFRA. One rule expanded the scope of exempt employers to include not only religious nonprofits like Little Sisters but any employer that has a sincere religious objection, including for-profit and publicly traded companies. The second rule exempted nonprofits and closely held for-profit organizations that objected to the mandate on moral grounds. The States of Pennsylvania and New Jersey challenged the new rules, arguing that neither the ACA nor RFRA authorized the exemptions and that in promulgating the rules the Departments failed to follow proper procedure, as spelled in the Administrative Procedure Act (APA).[9] The States prevailed in the district court and in the Court of Appeals for the Third Circuit.

With Justice Thomas writing for the Court, it overturned the Third Circuit. Everyone—the Departments, the States of Pennsylvania and New Jersey, the Third Circuit, and every member of the Court—agreed that the relevant section of the ACA requires health insurance plans for women to provide "preventive care and screenings... as provided for in comprehensive guidelines supported by the Health Resources and Services Administration," but of course they disagreed about the meaning of those words. The Third Circuit ruled that this language

---

[8] See *Zubik v. Burwell*, 578 U.S. __ (2016) (*per curiam*).
[9] On the role of the APA and its requirement for reasoned decision-making see Chapter 4 on the DACA case.

empowered the Departments to specify the preventive care and screenings to be provided but *not* to create exceptions from those requirements, something Justice Ginsburg argued in dissent (joined by Justice Sotomayor). The Court rejected this reading, finding that it was not supported by the language itself and that, moreover, Congress did not, as it has done in other statutes, give examples of services that had to be provided or supply criteria and standards for the Departments to follow. This meant the contested language gave "virtually unbridled discretion" to the Departments to define the required preventive care and screenings and to "identify and create exemptions from its own guidelines."[10] Because the Court found that the ACA empowered the Departments to make the exemptions, it did not need to decide whether RFRA *requires* the exemptions (though that also may be the case and would likely result in a judgment for the Little Sisters).

The Court likewise rejected the Third Circuit's conclusion that the Departments did not comply with the APA's procedural requirements. The arguments were that the Departments did not give adequate notice of proposed rulemaking, which meant that there was not sufficient opportunity for public comment, and that, because the final rules were almost identical to earlier interim rules, the Departments failed to maintain a "flexible and open-minded attitude" through the rulemaking process. The inadequate notice argument centered on the sufficiency of the title of the document issued to alert the public to, and invite comment on, departmental rulemaking. The Court held that the APA does not require documents to be titled in the way the Third Circuit ruled and, even if it did, it was harmless error, as irrespective of the title, the document fully explained the Departments' position and supplied the public with the chance to comment on the proposed regulations. As for the "open-mindedness" obligation, the Court ruled that this was a judge-made rule foreign to the APA; the text of the law is what counts, and the Departments had fully complied with it.

Justice Alito concurred (joined by Justice Gorsuch), adding that RFRA requires the exemption for Little Sisters and others with sincere religious objections: Because the contraceptive mandate substantially burdens the

---

[10] *Little Sisters* decision, pages 15–16.

exercise of religion, is not supported by a compelling interest, and is not narrowly tailored, it cannot stand under RFRA.

Justice Kagan concurred as well (joined by Justice Breyer), arguing that the ACA seems to give the agency just enough discretion to make those exemptions. However, Kagan questions whether the agency did follow all of the APA's requirements for "reasoned decisionmaking" and the avoidance of "arbitrary and capricious" rules. Kagan's point is that the Departments solved the limited problem of a small number of religious institutions with a broader solution that exempts even for-profit corporations with moral qualms. She argues that the lower courts must now decide if that violates the APA's requirement that "agencies must rationally account for their judgments."[11]

Future Implications

Espinoza is potentially the most momentous of the decisions, though it is not a surprising ruling given the Court's free exercise trajectory over the last several decades emphasizing equality between religion and nonreligion. Its significance is that it seemingly limits the rejection of state funding in *Locke v. Davey* to its specific facts of clergy education. In most public benefit schemes, religious service providers now appear to be on the same plane as secular providers. Many state constitutions have no-aid provisions like Montana's, which are now unenforceable, at least to the extent they discriminate on the basis of religious status. School funding is the policy realm in which *Espinoza* will likely be most strongly felt. States that provide financial assistance like vouchers and tax-credits for private schooling must include religious schools as well. How the logic of *Espinoza* applies to public schools and their funding is unknown. It could be argued that the ruling requires states to fund religious schooling on the same basis as their funding of secular public schools. Whether logic compels this conclusion or not, it's doubtful that a majority of Justices would reach such a transformative conclusion.

---

[11] Kagan concurrence page 7.

Lady of Guadalupe makes clear that whether an employee falls within the scope of the ministerial exception is to be decided by the totality of the circumstances, with the school's explanation of the teacher's role an important part of the evidentiary inquiry. Critics worry that religious schools will manipulate job descriptions to move all employment decisions beyond the reach of antidiscrimination law, while supporters believe that a strong version of the ministerial exception is needed to ensure the freedom to guide religious education.

And *Little Sisters of the Poor* may not be the final word on exemptions for religious institutions of various kinds. The combined—and sometimes competing—requirements of the First Amendment, the core healthcare law (ACA), the core administrative law (APA), and Congress' protection of religious liberty (RFRA), mean that future conflict and litigation may be inevitable.

6

Hernández v. Mesa on Rights and Restitution for Victims of Excessive Force at the Border

Paul M. Collins Jr. and Rebecca Hamlin

On June 7, 2010, Sergio Adrián Hernández Güereca, a 15-year-old Mexican national, was shot and killed on the Mexican side of the US/Mexico border by US Border Patrol Agent Jesus Mesa, Jr. According to Hernández's lawyers, the youth was playing a game with some friends that involved crossing a cement culvert that separates the two nations, briefly touching the US border, and running back to the Mexican side. According to Mesa, Hernández and his friends were trying to cross the border illegally and were throwing rocks at Mesa. Not in dispute is the fact that Mesa fired two shots at Hernández from the American side, one of which killed him on Mexican territory. This incident, which happened a decade ago, led to a Supreme Court case that combined two of the most inflammatory political issues of the Trump era—immigration enforcement and police brutality.

First, this cross-border killing became an international incident, with the US and Mexican governments disagreeing about how to handle the investigation, assess liability, and determine potential punishment. The

P. M. Collins Jr. (✉) · R. Hamlin
University of Massachusetts Amherst, Amherst, MA, USA

© The Author(s) 2021
M. Marietta (ed.), *SCOTUS 2020*,
https://doi.org/10.1007/978-3-030-53851-4_6

United States Department of Justice conducted an investigation and found that Mesa had not violated Customs and Border Protection (CBP) policies, and so the government did not bring criminal charges or other legal actions against Mesa. Unsatisfied with this investigation, Mexico requested that the United States extradite Mesa to face criminal charges in the Mexican judicial system. The United States refused this request.

Then, on January 17, 2011, Hernández's parents brought a lawsuit in the United States for damages against Mesa, arguing that he violated Hernández's Fourth and Fifth Amendment rights, along with a variety of other claims. The Fourth Amendment to the US Constitution states that "The right of the people to be secure in their persons, houses, papers, and effects, against unreasonable searches and seizures, shall not be violated." The Court has interpreted this Amendment to forbid the use of deadly force against a fleeing suspect, unless that suspect presented a serious threat to the safety of the officer or other individuals.[1] The Hernández's Fourth Amendment argument is that Officer Mesa was unjustified in his use of excessive force against their unarmed son.[2] The relevant portion of the Fifth Amendment reads, "No person shall … be deprived of life, liberty, or property, without due process of law." The Fifth Amendment claim is that Mesa violated Hernández's due process rights by killing him without the procedures required by the Fifth Amendment, such as the right to a trial by an unbiased jury.

In a variety of cases in the US District Court for the Western District of Texas and the US Court of Appeals for the Fifth Circuit, these claims were dismissed. Most notably, the Fifth Circuit held that the Fourth Amendment claim was invalid because Hernández was on Mexican soil at the time of the shooting and because he had no significant connection to the United States, putting him outside the scope of the Amendment's protection. The Fifth Circuit dismissed the Fifth Amendment claim on grounds that, as a Border Patrol Agent, Mesa was entitled to qualified immunity, which protects government officials from lawsuits for actions taken in their official capacities. Under the doctrine of qualified immunity, government agents are only liable if they intentionally

---

[1] See *Tennessee v. Garner*, 471 U.S. 1 (1985); *Graham v. Connor*, 490 U.S. 386 (1989).
[2] *Hernández* Petitioner's Brief, page 27.

and egregiously went beyond the scope of their job duties to violate a clearly recognized statutory or constitutional right.[3]

In a previous appearance of this dispute before the US Supreme Court in 2017, the Court asked the Fifth Circuit Court of Appeals to reconsider the case in light of the recent precedent in *Ziglar v. Abbasi* (2017), which upheld the qualified immunity doctrine in the context of the post-9/11 detentions of Arab Americans. In *Ziglar*, the Court revisited the precedent on which *Hernández v. Mesa* would rest: *Bivens v. Six Unknown Named Agents* (1971). In *Bivens*, federal narcotics agents entered Bivens' home without a warrant, and conducted a humiliating interrogation and search in front of his family. The case explored the question of what recourse was owed to him after the fact. The opinion of the Court set out the conditions under which individuals who believe their constitutional rights have been violated by federal government officials acting under the color of law can sue for damages in the absence of a federal law authorizing such suits—known thereafter as a *Bivens* claim.

Upon reconsidering the case in light of *Ziglar*, the Fifth Circuit determined that the Hernández's did not have a *Bivens* claim for several reasons, including Hernández's location on Mexican soil, the international affairs and national security aspects of the case, and Congress' refusal to legislate a remedy for killings that took place on foreign soil. The Supreme Court agreed to review the Fifth Circuit's decision on May 28, 2019.

The Constitutional Questions and Broader Political Meaning

This case revolves around two major constitutional issues. First is the question of who is eligible for rights protections under the US Constitution. This question was not at issue in *Bivens*, since he was a US citizen on US territory, but is central in *Hernández*. The circumstances under

---

[3]Recent precedents of the Court apply qualified immunity to "all but the plainly incompetent or those who knowingly violate the law" (*Malley v. Briggs*, 475 U.S. at 341, 1986), suggesting that "if a reasonable officer might not have known for certain that the conduct was unlawful—then the officer is immune from liability" (*Ziglar v. Abassi* [2017] decision, page 29).

which constitutional protections extend to noncitizens is a long-standing theme in American constitutional law. The Court has explicitly declined to extend rights to noncitizens who are outside the territory of the United States in a number of different cases.[4] However, none of these cases have dealt with a scenario in which the alleged rights *violator* was on US soil and was a US government agent. As the discussion below makes clear, the Justices deeply disagreed about how this unique situation affected Hernández's status as a rights-holding individual.

The second major issue in this case is the matter of recourse when someone has been harmed by an agent of the state. The Constitution is clear that there are limits on the actions of government actors, but not what individuals can do about it when those actors overstep their limits. *Bivens* inferred that the proper recourse was to allow individuals to sue for damages, but a majority of the current Justices are reluctant to expand the scope of such remedies to new scenarios. While the majority opinion goes to great lengths to divorce the case from the larger policy context, the outcome of the case has major ramifications for immigration enforcement and recourse for government abuses, issues at the core of our current politics.

The Majority Opinion

On February 25, 2020, the Court announced its decision. By a 5-4 vote down ideological and partisan lines, the Court's conservative majority— Alito, Gorsuch, Kavanaugh, Roberts, and Thomas—held that *Bivens* does not apply to cross-border shootings. Therefore, the Hernández family has no legal remedy in the United States to address the killing of their 15-year-old son.

Writing for the Court, Justice Alito's majority opinion focused almost entirely on the application of *Bivens*. In order to apply *Bivens* to the current case and allow the Hernández's claim to move forward, Alito

---

[4]See, for example, *Sale v. Haitian Centers Council*, 509 U.S. 155 (1993), *Leng May Ma v. Barber*, 357 U.S. 185 (1958), *Shaughnessy v. U.S. ex rel Mezei*, 345 U.S. 206 (1953), and *Ekiu v. United States*, 142 U.S. 651 (1892).

wrote, the Court must use a two-step process. First, the Court must determine if the claim arises in a "new context" from previous *Bivens* claims. If it does, the Court must address a second inquiry: whether there are "special factors" that compel hesitation in authorizing a *Bivens* claim.[5]

With regard to the question of whether the *Bivens* claim related to a "new context," the Court's majority found it did. Alito compared the claim in this case to four other *Bivens* claims it had previously addressed. These involved an allegation of sex discrimination in Washington, D.C., an allegedly unconstitutional arrest in New York City, the failure to provide medical treatment in an Indiana prison, and a suit against a private prison operator. Alito argued that there is a "world of difference between" those precedents and the cross-border killing at issue in this case, especially given the international dimension.[6] The Court noted four concerns that suggested authorizing the *Bivens* claim would be unwise.

First, the Court argued that allowing a *Bivens* claim in this case might have an effect on international relations, an area traditionally left to the executive and legislative branches of government, not the judiciary. According to Alito, "a cross-border shooting is by definition an international incident," and thus the Court's majority felt it unwise to become involved in the dispute.[7] In Alito's view, it was not the Court's job to arbitrate between two nations on a matter of international affairs.

Second, the Court determined that this case involves a matter of national security. Because illegal border crossings may involve drug trafficking, human smuggling, and other forms of illegality, Agent Mesa's conduct has a connection to national security concerns. Similar to international relations between governments, national security of the US border is traditionally a matter for the elected branches of government.

Third, the Court was reluctant to recognize a *Bivens* claim because Congress failed to authorize it to do so. Alito highlighted that when Congress considered damage claims for violations of constitutional rights by *state* officials, they intentionally limited claims to those made by citizens of the United States or those within US jurisdiction (U.S. Code

---

[5] *Hernández* decision, page 7.
[6] Ibid. at 8.
[7] Ibid. at 9.

Title 42, Section 1983). Because Congress set up such a limitation, and since Hernández was a Mexican national, the Court reasoned that it would be unwise to expand *Bivens* to cover claims against federal officials made by those outside of US jurisdiction.

Finally, Alito concluded the majority opinion by arguing that extending *Bivens* to cover cross-border killings in the absence of any congressional authorization would violate the separation of powers. In essence, Alito boils down the previous three points regarding the Court's unwillingness to extend *Bivens* by arguing that it is not the proper role of the judicial branch to make decisions in the realm of foreign affairs: "the most important question 'is 'who should decide' whether to provide for a damages remedy, Congress or the courts?' The correct 'answer most often will be Congress'."[8] In other words, the proper institution to determine whether to allow damages for cross-border shootings is Congress, not the courts.

In reading the Court's opinion, it is clear that the conservative Justices in the majority are quite critical of *Bivens* itself, not merely its application or expansion in this case. For example, Alito notes the Court "broke new ground" in *Bivens*, and that the decision was the product "of an era when the Court routinely inferred 'causes of action' that were 'not explicit' in the text of the provision that was allegedly violated."[9] In other words, Justice Alito and the Court's majority view *Bivens* as a form of judicial activism, expanding the Court's authority in matters traditionally left to the legislative branch. Although the majority did not overrule *Bivens*, it is reasonable to infer that this precedent may be on its way out if some of the Justices in the conservative majority get their way in future cases.

The Concurring Opinion

Revealing what may eventually be in store for the *Bivens* doctrine, Justice Thomas wrote a brief concurring opinion, joined by Justice Gorsuch. Thomas argues that the basic notion of *Bivens*—the idea that causes of

---

[8] Ibid. at 19–20, quoting *Ziglar v. Abassi* (2017), quoting *Bush v. Lucas* (1983).
[9] Ibid. at 4, quoting *Ziglar v. Abassi* (2017).

action against federal officers can be judicially created when they are merely implied by statute—should be abandoned as bad precedent. In his view, *Bivens* grants far too much legislative power to courts, allowing the judiciary to create causes of action that go beyond what legislators imagined. Thomas concludes that *Bivens* is a relic of a bygone era of judicial overreach, even suggesting that officially overruling *Bivens* would not be much more than a housecleaning because the Court has been distancing itself from the logic of *Bivens* for several decades.

The Dissenting Opinion

Justice Ginsburg wrote the dissenting opinion in the case, which was joined by Justices Breyer, Kagan, and Sotomayor. In contrast to the majority, Ginsburg finds that the context arising in this case is not new and distinct from previous scenarios in which the Court applied *Bivens*. Rather, she calls the context "familiar" and argues that the location of the unarmed subject "should not matter one whit."[10] She points out that Officer Mesa was on US soil and subject to US law when he used lethal force against an unarmed subject: whether his bullet landed on one side or the other of the border was "happenstance."[11]

While the majority argues that allowing the Hernández family to bring a damages action would affect the US/Mexico relationship, Ginsburg points out that there will also be a diplomatic ripple effect of telling the family that there is no recourse. She notes that the Mexican government raises this exact point in its *amicus curiae* ("friend of the court") brief in support of the Hernández family. She also notes that allowing a *Bivens* action would be consistent with the right to compensation outlined in the International Covenant on Civil and Political Rights, which the United States has ratified.

In regard to the national security argument made in the majority opinion, Ginsburg states that she fails to grasp what precise national security concern would be raised by allowing a damages action against an

---

[10] *Hernández* Ginsburg dissent, pages 2, 7.
[11] Ibid. at 8.

individual officer who is alleged to have committed an unjustified killing. She also points to other instances, some outlined in the briefs, of cross-border shootings by Border Patrol agents, suggesting that this incident is part of a larger pattern. She cites a report by a nonpartisan Washington D.C. think tank, the American Immigration Council, which analyzed data from 2009–2012 and found an ongoing pattern of excessive force and other forms of physical, verbal, and sexual abuse.[12]

Concluding that the circumstances of the case are similar enough to *Bivens* for that precedent to apply, Ginsburg considers the question of remedy. Summarizing the background of the *Bivens* case, Ginsburg argues that even though Congress had not expressly outlined such a provision, monetary damages are the only available remedy for dealing with federal agents who have overstepped constitutional bounds. As in *Bivens*, and unlike the *Ziglar v. Abbasi* decision in which the Court declined to apply *Bivens* to the context of immigration detention, the Hernández family has no recourse to alternative remedies, which Ginsburg argues should be a "significant consideration."[13] She concludes that "to redress injuries like the one suffered here, it is *Bivens* or nothing. I resist the conclusion that 'nothing' is the answer required in this case."[14]

In sum, the Ginsburg dissent outlines a markedly different view of the case. It is focused on protecting the rights of victims to redress, regardless of their country of origin, and on disincentivizing the overreach of state authority. To the question of whether these protections constitute judicial activism, she points out that Congress has been aware of *Bivens* remedies for decades and has not taken legislative action to prevent them.

---

[12]Martinez, Daniel E., Guillermo Cantor, and Walter A. Ewing, "No Action Taken: Lack of CBP Accountability in Responding to Complaints of Abuse," *American Immigration Council* (Washington, DC, 2014).

[13]Ibid. at 9.

[14]*Hernández* Ginsburg dissent, page 14.

Conclusion

The question of recourse when government agents abuse their authority or employ excessive—even deadly—force is an extremely timely one. While the touchstone in contemporary American politics has been the issue of racialized police brutality, there is evidence of a systemic problem with abuse by Border Patrol agents as well. The dissent does not cite it, but a follow-up report by the American Immigration Council found that the pattern it exposed in 2014 has not improved, and that even after Customs and Border Protection was made aware of the problem, in 96% of cases CBP took no action against the agent accused of wrong-doing.[15] This issue of excessive force by government agents has received less media attention than police brutality, perhaps in part because the actions of Border Patrol agents are less public, and also perhaps because their victims are almost always noncitizens. But it is clear that Border Patrol agents frequently abuse their power, and that CBP does not have systems in place to hold those agents accountable.

In many ways, this case came down to the question of what, if anything, courts can do about this worrisome problem. In doing so, it combined two major hot button partisan issues of the Trump administration: immigration enforcement and policy brutality. Perhaps unsurprisingly then, given the highly fraught politics of both issues, the 5-4 decision represents another classic ideological and partisan split among the Justices. The conservative members of the Court all signed onto a majority opinion that is focused almost entirely on a narrow interpretation of the law designed to limit judicial power, and without an expressed regard for the policy consequences of their decision. In contrast, the liberal Justices joined a dissenting opinion that stakes out a very different view, one that highlights the question of justice for the Hernández family as well as the larger policy context and the role of legal action in achieving social change.

---

[15]Cantor, Guillermo, and Ewing, "Still No Action Taken: Complaints Against Border Patrol Agents Continue to Go Unanswered," *American Immigration Council* (Washington, DC, 2017), 16.

The *Hernández* decision serves as an indicator of where the Roberts Courts may be headed on more general questions of excessive force and immigration enforcement. Their position was further clarified on June 15, 2020, when the Court declined to review a group of cases regarding the doctrine of qualified immunity.[16] This denial of certiorari suggests that a majority of the Court expects Congress to act if qualified immunity is to be reformed. Similarly, they expect Congress to act if victims of excessive force at the border are to be given any recourse. Finally, the Court's June 25, 2020 decision in *Department of Homeland Security v. Thuraissigiam* also gave a clue as to their position on rights for individuals who are just over the border on the US side.[17] The five conservative Justices signed onto Alito's majority opinion, which implied that because Thuraissigiam had entered illegally and was only a few yards across the border for a few moments, he had no rights to due process. The question of how far into the United States a person must travel, and for how long, in order to qualify for constitutional protection remains to be seen.

---

[16] *Baxter v. Bracey* et al., on petition for writ of certiorari to the United States Court of Appeals for the Sixth Circuit, No. 18–1287. Decided 15 June 2020.

[17] *Department of Homeland Security v. Thuraissigiam*, 591 U.S. __ (2020).

7

June Medical Services v. Russo on State Regulation of Abortion Clinics

Gerald N. Rosenberg

The constitutional law of abortion is deeply entwined with the politics of abortion. When the Supreme Court issued its opinion in *June Medical Services*, striking down a Louisiana law regulating abortion clinics, it did so in the context of decades of political and legal conflict.

The Law and Politics of Abortion

In 1973, nearly fifty years ago, the Supreme Court held in *Roe v. Wade* that a pregnant woman, in consultation with her physician, had a constitutional right to terminate an unwanted pregnancy with no or minimal state interference for the first two trimesters (two thirds) of

G. N. Rosenberg (✉)
University of Chicago, Chicago, IL, USA

© The Author(s) 2021
M. Marietta (ed.), *SCOTUS 2020*,
https://doi.org/10.1007/978-3-030-53851-4_7

her pregnancy.[1] The 1973 decision mirrored public opinion.[2] Over the succeeding decades, tens of millions of women have had legal abortions and public support for a woman's choice has remained remarkably steady or has increased. In May 2020, the month before the Supreme Court issued its opinion in *June Medical Services*, Gallup found that only twenty percent of respondents thought that abortion should be illegal in all circumstances compared to seventy-nine percent of respondents who told Gallup abortion should be legal in all or certain circumstances.[3] Other pollsters have reported similar findings.

Alongside majority support for safe and legal abortion, an intense minority has mobilized to limit abortion and overturn *Roe v. Wade*. Abortion opponents have picketed abortion clinics, protested at the Supreme Court, and lobbied Congress and state legislatures to restrict or ban abortion. Abortion has figured prominently in Senate hearings on Supreme Court nominations. Politically, there is a large partisan divide in views on abortion. In May 2020 Gallup reported that nearly four times as many Democrats as Republicans believe that abortion should be legal under any circumstances and more than three times as many Republicans as Democrats believe that abortion should be illegal in all circumstances.[4] This partisan divide matters because in the years since *Roe,* Republican presidents have appointed eleven of the fifteen Justices who have served on the Supreme Court.

There is also debate about whether the Constitution protects the right to an abortion. *Roe* is grounded in a right of privacy the Court found in the Due Process Clause of the Fourteenth Amendment ("nor shall any State deprive any person of life, liberty, or property, without due process of law"). Critics argue that no such right exists, which means that the legality of abortion is a matter for state legislatures to decide rather than the Court. If *Roe* were overturned, many states would maintain legality, a few would likely outlaw abortion, and others would impose various restrictions. The specific question in many cases like *June Medical*

---

[1]410 U.S. 113 (1973).
[2]Gerald N. Rosenberg, *The Hollow Hope: Can Courts Bring About Social Change?* 2nd Ed. (Chicago: University of Chicago Press, 2008).
[3]Lynda Saad, "Americans' Abortion Views Steady in Past Year," *Gallup* (29 June 2020).
[4]Ibid.

is whether a given regulation is allowable, but the broader question of whether the Court will overturn *Roe* always lurks in the background.

In the decades after *Roe*, the Supreme Court heard dozens of cases challenging abortion regulations that limited but didn't completely ban it. In 1992, in *Planned Parenthood of Southeastern Pennsylvania v. Casey*, the Supreme Court adopted the "undue burden" standard for judging the constitutionality of abortion regulations:

> An undue burden exists, and therefore a provision of law is invalid, if its purpose or effect is to place a substantial obstacle in the path of a woman seeking an abortion before the fetus attains viability.[5]

The decision left unanswered what exactly constitutes an "undue burden" and what is an allowable regulation.

In 2016, the Court heard a challenge to a Texas law requiring doctors working at abortion clinics to have admitting privileges at a hospital within 30 miles and requiring clinics to meet the strict standards for ambulatory surgical centers. Texas defended the law as designed to protect the health and safety of women seeking abortions. Critics argued that the law was unnecessary to protect women's health and was designed to make it harder for women to obtain abortions. In *Whole Woman's Health v. Hellerstedt* the Court invalidated the law. Writing for the majority, Justice Breyer wrote that "neither of these provisions offers medical benefits sufficient to justify the burdens upon access that each imposes. Each places a substantial obstacle in the path of women seeking a previability abortion, each constitutes an undue burden on abortion access, and each violates the federal Constitution."[6]

Since *Roe* no state has enacted more laws restricting abortion than Louisiana. In June 2014, the state adopted Act 620. Virtually identical to the Texas law, Act 620 required that doctors performing abortions have "active admitting privileges at a hospital that is located not further than thirty miles from the location at which the abortion is performed or induced and that provides obstetrical or gynecological health care

---

[5] *Planned Parenthood v. Casey*, 505 U.S. 833 (1992) at 878.
[6] *Whole Woman's Health v. Hellerstedt*, 579 U.S. ___ (2016) at 2.

services." When the law was passed there were five abortion providers in the state. By the time of the Supreme Court case there were only three.

Briefs and Oral Argument

The Supreme Court heard oral arguments on March 4, 2020. Illustrating the political importance of the case, seventy *amicus* briefs were filed, forty-three by supporters of the law and twenty-seven by opponents. One brief supporting the law was filed by 207 members of Congress, signed by 39 Republican Senators and 168 House members. Only two of the 168 House signers were Democrats, one of whom lost his primary in 2020 to a pro-choice opponent. In opposition to the law, a brief was filed by 197 Members of Congress comprised of 36 Democratic Senators and 161 Democratic House Members. Twenty-one states plus Washington, D.C. field a brief in support of the clinic and twenty-two states filed briefs supporting Louisiana. Nearly 200 hundred major national organizations filed briefs. The list included the American Medical Association, the American College of Obstetricians and Gynecologists, the American Academy of Pediatrics, and the American Bar Association, all in support of the clinic.

In both its brief and oral argument, the plaintiffs stressed the importance of following precedent and deferring to the district court's finding of facts. At the start of its brief, the plaintiffs wrote: "A properly functioning legal system depends on certain basic operating principles. One is the maxim that legal holdings of higher courts are binding on lower courts. Another is that a trial court's factual findings govern on appeal unless clearly erroneous."[7] The brief argued that "Louisiana's admitting-privileges law is materially indistinguishable from the Texas law the Court invalidated in *Whole Woman's Health*" and that "*Whole Woman's Health* controls this case."[8] The first sentence that the clinic's lawyer, Julie Rikelman, stated in oral argument made the same point: "This case

---

[7] Brief for Petitioners, *June Medical Services v. Russo*, page 2.
[8] Ibid. at 17, 21.

is about respect for the Court's precedent."[9] The brief also argued that because the admitting-privileges law confers "*no* health or safety benefit, the burdens Act 620 imposes are necessarily undue."[10]

In response Louisiana filed a 90-page brief! The state argued that the clinics and doctors lacked standing to bring the suit, that the district court's fact-finding was inadequate, and that the judge misapplied the law. The state argued that the Louisiana law was different from the Texas law struck down in *Whole Woman's Health* and therefore that decision was not binding: "In this case the record shows not only that the challenged law serves specific public-health needs in Louisiana, but that the law's alleged burdens are illusory."[11] The point was reiterated in oral argument where Elizabeth Murrill, arguing for Louisiana, said, "The law was different, the facts are different. The regulatory structure is different. And the record is different. And all of those things dictated a different result."[12] In addition, in its brief, the state argued that the correct constitutional question was not whether the law created any benefit but rather whether it created a substantial obstacle to women seeking abortions. The state argued that a proper factual analysis showed that it didn't.

There were two important issues lurking in the background. One was if the Court would use the case to overturn *Roe v. Wade*. With the replacement of Justice Kennedy with Justice Kavanaugh, it was widely thought that there was a majority of five Republican-appointed Justices opposed to the constitutional right to abortion. The second issue was timing. The case would be decided in a presidential election year. While a decision invalidating the law would upset antiabortion activists, a decision upholding the law would upset the much larger pro-choice constituency. A national poll taken in late April and early May, 2020, before the case was decided, found that fifty-seven percent of respondents believed that it was a violation of a woman's constitutional right for a state to require doctors who provide abortions to have hospital admitting privileges. Seventy-three percent of Democrats took this position

---

[9] *June Medical Services v. Russo* oral arguments transcript, 4 March 2020, page 4.
[10] Brief for Petitioners, page 47.
[11] Brief for the Respondent/Cross-Petitioner, pages 1–2.
[12] *June Medical Services v. Russo* oral arguments transcript, 4 March 2020, page 33.

as did fifty-six percent of Independents.[13] If the Court were to uphold the law then Democrats would surely increase attacks on the Court during the campaign. Historically, the Court has not fared well when it becomes entangled with presidential politics, especially if opponents to major decisions win.[14]

The decision was announced late in the Court's term, on June 29th. It covers 138 pages. There are six separate opinions. Justice Breyer wrote for the Court and for three of his colleagues, Justices Ginsburg, Kagan, and Sotomayor. Chief Justice John Roberts filed a concurring opinion in which he agreed that the Louisiana law should be struck down but not for the reasons Justice Breyer gave. The four conservative Justices each wrote dissenting opinions. Given the length, complexity, and richness of the opinions, the following discussion only highlights important points.

The decision revolves around four key issues. First is the issue of standing to sue, whether the doctors and clinics could challenge the law on the ground that it created an undue burden on women seeking to exercise their constitutional right to an abortion by placing a substantial obstacle in their way. The doctors and clinics were not themselves seeking abortions and thus were "third parties" in the relationship between women seeking abortions and the state.

Second is the question of whether the Court was bound by the doctrine of precedent to follow its decision in the Texas case in 2016. Third is the application of the undue burden standard. Fourth is the standard for examining the factual determinations made by the federal district judge who first heard the case. Surprisingly for a Supreme Court decision, much of the discussion in the opinions is taken up with conflicting interpretations of the facts.

Justice Breyer's plurality opinion for the Court (an opinion for the Court lacking at least five Justices is referred to as a "plurality" opinion) addressed each of the issues, albeit at different lengths. His underlying argument was the need to follow precedent. On page two he describes

---

[13]Adam Liptak and Alicia Parlapiano, "The Major Supreme Court Cases This Term and What the Public Thinks," *The New York Times* (15 June 2020).

[14]Gerald N. Rosenberg, "Judicial Independence and the Reality of Political Power," *Review of Politics* 54: 369–398 (1992).

the Louisiana law as "almost word-for-word identical to Texas' admitting-privileges law."[15] Throughout his opinion he uses the word "identical" either by itself or modified by adjectives such as "substantially," "facially," and "nearly" five times.[16] He concludes: "This case is similar to, nearly identical with, *Whole Woman's Health*. And the law must consequently reach a similar conclusion. Act 620 is unconstitutional."[17]

Justice Breyer had little trouble finding that the doctors had standing to challenge the law. He noted that at the beginning of judicial proceedings in 2014, Louisiana's lawyers stated that there was "no question that the physicians had standing to contest the law."[18] The state didn't raise its objection to the plaintiff's standing until the Supreme Court agreed to hear the case, more than five years later. Thus, Breyer concludes, the state was barred from raising it now.

Justice Breyer spent many pages discussing the facts, which are critical to a claim of an undue burden: Does the law in fact impose an obstacle? Do the regulations in fact provide a medical benefit? Breyer quotes from the Federal Rules of Civil Procedure which state that a district court's finding of facts "must not be set aside unless clearly erroneous." Finally, Breyer reiterated that the constitutional standard articulated in *Whole Woman's Health* for judging the constitutionality of abortion regulations required judges to "weigh the law's 'asserted benefits against the burdens' it imposes on abortion access." Because the district court's finding of facts was "not clearly erroneous," Breyer upheld "its determination that Louisiana's law poses a 'substantial obstacle' to women seeking an abortion; its determination that the law offers no significant health-related benefits; and its determination that the law consequently imposes an 'undue burden' on a woman's constitutional right to choose to have an abortion."[19]

The late Justice William Brennan reportedly would tell his clerks that the most important thing to know about the Supreme Court was the number five. Presumably he meant that with five votes the Court could

---

[15] *June Medical* Breyer plurality, page 2.
[16] Ibid. at 2, 3, 12, 25 and 40.
[17] Ibid. at 40.
[18] Ibid. at 12.
[19] Ibid. at 17, 2, and 38.

make a binding decision. Breyer's opinion was only joined by three other Justices. To invalidate the Louisiana law he needed a fifth vote.

The fifth vote came from a surprising source, Chief Justice Roberts. His concurring opinion to strike down the Louisiana law was surprising because he had dissented in *Whole Woman's Health* where he would have upheld the Texas law requiring admitting privileges. Indeed, he writes on page two of his opinion that he "continue[s] to believe that the case was wrongly decided."[20] Why, then, did he write a concurring opinion striking down the Louisiana law? Legally, he provides a reason; adherence to precedent (*stare decisis*). "The question" in this case, he writes, "is not whether *Whole Woman's Health* was right or wrong, but whether to adhere to it in deciding the present case."[21] Quoting from *Black's Law Dictionary*, Blackstone's *Commentaries on the Laws of England*, Burke's *Reflections on the Revolution in France*, and *Federalist 78*, Roberts writes that the "legal doctrine of *stare decisis* requires us, absent special circumstances, to treat like cases alike."[22] Three times in his opinion he describes the Louisiana law as "nearly identical" to the Texas law.[23] Thus, he writes, "[u]nder principles of *stare decisis*, I agree with the plurality that the determination in *Whole Woman's Health* that Texas's law imposed a substantial obstacle requires the same determination about Louisiana's law."[24]

Why, then, did he write a concurring opinion and not join Breyer's opinion? The reason, it appears, is that Breyer's opinion relies on balancing the purported benefits of the law with the burden it creates. For Chief Justice Roberts, this is a misreading of *Casey* which, he writes, "looked to whether there was a substantial burden, not whether benefits outweighed burdens."[25]

There may be another reason why Chief Justice Roberts concurred in the opinion: politics. As noted above, 2020 is a presidential election year and a decision upholding the Louisiana law would have been both

---

[20] Roberts concurrence, page 2.
[21] Ibid. See the discussion of precedent in Chapter 12 by David Klein on the *Ramos* ruling.
[22] Ibid.
[23] Ibid. at 2, 12, 16.
[24] Ibid. at 11.
[25] Ibid. at 8.

unpopular and likely to insert the Court into the presidential campaign. It is plausible that from his perspective Roberts made the best of a bad situation by voting to strike down the law while preventing five votes for a balancing test for abortion regulations.

The Dissents

There were four dissents in the case written by Justices Thomas, Alito, Gorsuch, and Kavanaugh. The longest dissent by far (34 pages) was written by Alito, who launched a broadside against the decision, writing that it "twists the law." In both *Whole Women's Health* and this decision, Alito wrote, "the abortion right recognized in this Court's decisions is used like a bulldozer to flatten legal rules that stand in the way." In particular, he argued that doctors who provide abortions are interested in making money and avoiding regulations whereas women seeking abortions are interested in their safety. This "blatant conflict of interest" precluded the doctors from asserting the rights of women wishing to obtain an abortion as the basis of their standing. "[I]t is deeply offensive to our rules of standing," Alito wrote, "to permit them to sue in the name of their patients when they challenge laws enacted to protect their patients' safety."[26]

Alito also argued that the plurality misapplied the undue burden standard by balancing the benefits of the law against the burden created. The correct constitutional standard, he argued, was "*Casey's* 'substantial obstacle' test, not the *Whole Woman's Health* balancing test," and hence *Whole Woman's Health* should be overruled.[27]

Like Breyer's opinion, Alito's dissent was heavily fact-based. In his view, the opinion of the federal district judge striking down the law was based on a "thoroughly inadequate factual inquiry." Alito found "ample evidence in the record showing that requiring admitting privileges has

---

[26]Alito dissent, pages 34, 1, 25, and 33–34.
[27]Ibid. at 24.

health and safety benefits."[28] In Alito's view, such factual determinations are best left to legislatures, not courts.

As for the issue of precedent, Alito found the two cases "very different." Admitting that it is "certainly true that the Texas and Louisiana *statutes* are largely the same," Alito maintained that the "two cases are not."[29] This was because of factual differences between Texas and Louisiana that Judge deGravelles failed to examine. Thus, the holding in *Whole Woman's Health* didn't require the Court to invalidate the Louisiana law.

Justice Thomas agreed with all of Alito's criticisms. He wrote separately for two reasons. First, he would have dismissed the case for lack of standing. Second, Thomas emphasized that there was no constitutional right to abortion. He concluded his dissent on these two points: "Because we lack jurisdiction and our abortion jurisprudence finds no basis in the Constitution, I respectfully dissent."[30]

Justice Gorsuch also wrote a dissent. Like Alito and Thomas, he objected to the granting of standing to the doctors. In addition to misapplying the Court's third-party standing rules, Gorsuch also argued that the Court violated other long-standing practices such as legislative deference. Like Alito, Gorsuch emphasized that the plurality assumed *Whole Woman's Health*'s "fact-laden predictions about how a Texas law would impact the availability of abortion in that State in 2016 … obviously and necessarily applied to Louisiana in 2020." In particular, he wrote that the plurality took a "remarkably static view of the market" that took no account of how hospitals might change their rules to offer admitting privileges, new providers with admitting privileges might start providing abortion services, and out-of-state abortion providers might move to Louisiana to meet the demand. The plurality's analysis, Gorsuch concluded, "is a sign we have lost our way."[31]

Finally, Justice Kavanaugh wrote a two-page dissent. Noting that five Justices rejected the balancing test of *Whole Woman's Health* (the

---

[28]Ibid. at 2, 8.
[29]Ibid. at 9.
[30]Thomas dissent, page 20.
[31]Gorsuch dissent, pages 14, 12, and 21.

dissenters plus Chief Justice Roberts), Kavanaugh argued that "additional factfinding is necessary to properly evaluate Louisiana's law."[32]

The Future

June Medical Services v. Russo resolved the issue of the constitutionality of Louisiana's law, finding it nearly identical to the Texas law struck down in 2016. It did not make new law and it did not resolve the question of what other abortion regulations are constitutional. At the time of the decision there were at least sixteen abortion cases in the lower federal courts. It is likely that one or more of them will make their way to the Supreme Court. And when they do, it is likely that the opinions of most of the Justices will coincide with the party of the president who appointed them. In the long run, then, the constitutional future of abortion is largely dependent on the political process and on which political party is able to make future Supreme Court appointments. Politics, rather than legal argument, will determine the future of the constitutional right to abortion.

---

[32]Kavanaugh dissent, page 2.

8

Kahler v. Kansas on the Insanity Defense

Julia Bess Frank and Mark A. Graber

President John F. Kennedy captured a fundamental difference between modern times and the framing era when he informed Nobel Laureates at a White House dinner that they were "the most extraordinary collection of talent, of human knowledge, that has ever been gathered together at the White House, with the possible exception of when Thomas Jefferson dined alone."[1] Jefferson lived at a time when leading constitutional decision makers could be leading authorities on history, science, medicine, and numerous other matters. "Jefferson was a gentleman of 32," Kennedy pointed out, "who could calculate an eclipse, survey an

---

[1]John F. Kennedy, "Remarks at a Dinner Honoring Nobel Prize Winners of the Western Hemisphere," *American Presidency Project* https://www.presidency.ucsb.edu/documents/remarks-dinner-honoring-nobel-prize-winners-the-western-hemisphere.

J. B. Frank (✉)
George Washington University School of Medicine and Health Sciences, Washington, DC, DC, USA

M. A. Graber
University of Maryland Carey School of Law, Baltimore, MD, USA

© The Author(s) 2021
M. Marietta (ed.), *SCOTUS 2020*,
https://doi.org/10.1007/978-3-030-53851-4_8

estate, tie an artery, plan an edifice, try a cause, break a horse, and dance the minuet." The development of disciplines ushered in the contemporary era of specialists. We do not expect government officials today to be the leading authority on any body of knowledge outside their narrow purview. We nevertheless expect them to decide constitutional law questions whose answers seem to require some social and physical science expertise.

Kahler v. Kansas challenged Supreme Court Justices who inherited from their enlightenment ancestors the responsibility of making constitutional decisions, but not their range of intellectual expertise. In order to decide whether Kansas could abolish the insanity defense in significant part, the Justices had to examine constitutional law (on which they presumably have considerable expertise), legal history (on which they might be considered gifted amateurs), and psychiatry (on which they have no expertise at all). The 6-3 decision sustaining a Kansas law that imposes criminal liability on persons who did not understand their actions were immoral relied on broadly acceptable constitutional law and problematic history, while attempting to leave psychiatric questions to state legislatures. By failing to discuss contemporary understandings of depression, both the majority and dissenting opinions failed to grapple fully with how the contemporary insanity defense approved by state legislators too often remains yoked to psychiatric understandings long since abandoned by medical practitioners.

James Kraig Kahler murdered his estranged spouse, his spouse's grandmother and his two daughters on Saturday, November 28, 2009.[2] At trial, Kahler conceded that he fired the fatal shots, but contended that he should be found not guilty by reason of insanity. A psychiatrist testifying for the defense diagnosed Kahler with severe major depression and claimed that "his capacity to manage his own behavior had been severely degraded so that he couldn't refrain from doing what he did." Psychiatrists testifying for the prosecution insisted that, despite Kahler's condition, he was capable of pre-mediation and forming an intent to kill. That was sufficient under Kansas law, which limits the insanity defense

---

[2]The facts in this paragraph are taken from the opinion in *State v. Kahler*, 307 Kan. 374 (2018).

to defendants who, "as a result of mental disease or defect, lacked the mental state required"—in other words, intent—"as an element of the offense charged." "Mental disease or defect," the law clearly states, "is not otherwise a defense."[3] Kahler was found guilty and sentenced to death. The Supreme Court of Kansas rejected Kahler's claim that the Kansas law violated the Due Process Clause of the Fourteenth Amendment by unduly restricting the insanity defense. Kahler appealed this decision to the Supreme Court. Due process, in his view, encompassed a basic principle of justice that forbade states from imposing criminal liability on persons who could not appreciate the morality of their conduct.

Constitutional Law

Kahler is the rare case in which both the majority and dissenting opinions were written by Justices on the liberal wing of the Roberts Court. One consequence of this phenomenon is the absence of "trash talk" which characterizes too many contemporary Supreme Court opinions.[4] Another is the agreement on the general principles underlying claims that a state law denies criminal defendants due process of law. Justice Elena Kagan's majority opinion and Justice Stephen Breyer's dissent maintained that state rules of criminal liability were unconstitutional only if they offend "some principle of justice so rooted in the traditions and conscience of our people as to be ranked as fundamental."[5] The relevant inquiry, both Justices agreed, was historical. Kagan noted, "The question is whether a rule of criminal responsibility is so old and venerable—so entrenched in the central values of our legal system—so as to prevent a State from ever choosing another."[6]

---

[3] K.S.A. 21-5209.
[4] See Sanford Levinson, "Trash Talk at the Supreme Court: Reflections on David Pozen's Constitutional Good Faith," 129 *Harvard Law Review Forum* 166 (2016).
[5] *Kahler* decision, page 10; Breyer dissent at 1.
[6] *Kahler* decision at 7.

Legal History

The discussions of legal history in the majority opinion and dissent found much common ground. Kagan and Breyer agreed that states had historically relied on various and different factors when determining when to find a criminal defendant not guilty by reason of insanity. Kagan identified at least five different versions of the insanity defense. States explored (1) "cognitive capacity," whether a defendant was "unable to understand what he was doing," (2) "moral capacity," whether a defendant was "unable to understand that his action was wrong," (3) legal capacity, whether a defendant was unable to understand that his action was illegal, (4) "volitional incapacity," whether a defendant was "unable to control his actions," or (5) a more broadly defined "product-of-mental-illness test" that "considers whether the defendant's criminal act stemmed from a mental disease."[7] Both opinions acknowledged that *M'Naghtens Case*, an 1843 English precedent, provided the benchmark for determining insanity in most states throughout most of American history. Lord Tindal in that case stated that for a judge or jury to find a defendant not guilty by reason of insanity, "it must be clearly proved that at the time of committing the act the party accused was labouring under such a defect of reason, from disease of the mind, as not to know the nature and quality of the act he was doing, or as not to know that what he was doing was wrong."[8]

Kagan maintained Kahler could not take shelter under *M'Naghten* because while many state courts adopted Lord Tindal's understanding of insanity, the common law in the United States and England before the nineteenth century did not regard moral incapacity as an affirmative defense and the status of moral incapacity remained contested long after *M'Naghten*. Such celebrated common law treatise writers as Henry de Bracton, Sir Edward Coke, Sir Matthew Hale, and Sir William Blackstone, Kagan claimed, limited the insanity defense to cognitive incapacity (intent). Many American jurisdictions never adopted or later abandoned *M'Naghten*. Kagan placed particular emphasis on contemporary state

---

[7] Ibid. at 2.
[8] *M'Naghten's Case*, 10 Cl. & Fin. 200,210, 8 Eng. Rep. 718, 722 (H. L. 1843).

laws that limit the insanity defense to persons who are unaware that their acts are illegal rather than immoral. That distinction, in her view, captures the difference between murderers who did not know the law and murderers who believed they were "commanded by God."[9] Kahler could not be convicted if the jury thought that because of his mental condition he did not realize he was firing a gun, her opinion suggested. Nevertheless, the weight of this history belied Kahler's claim that the Constitution commanded his acquittal because his mental condition did not enable him to realize that aiming a gun at live human beings was immoral.

Breyer disputed Kagan's characterization of both the common law and contemporary state law. His opinion maintained that the prominent common law treatise writers had uniformly recognized that persons who did not appreciate the morality of their actions could not be subject to criminal liability. Breyer insisted the verbal difference between state laws that require defendants to prove that they did not appreciate the *legality* of their conduct and state laws that require defendants to prove that they did not appreciate the *morality* of their conduct did not make a legal difference. "The two inquiries," he wrote, "are closely related and excuse roughly the same universe of defendants."[10] A murderer who does not appreciate that shooting four people in cold blood is illegal is not likely to appreciate that shooting four people in cold blood is immoral.

Breyer's dissent claims Kagan failed to understand that common law treatise writers did not make the sharp distinction between cognitive and moral capacity that had become common by the time *M'Nagthen* was decided. Only when we understand the mental universe of old English treatise writers can we appreciate that Bracton, Coke, Hale, and Blackstone were concerned with moral capacity, even if they did not express this concern in contemporary language. Just as Madison was not using "democracy" in a contemporary sense when in *Federalist* 10 he distinguished between democratic and representative governments, so Breyer claims that common law treatise writers used the Latin phrase "mens rea" to cover "general moral blameworthiness," while contemporary lawyers

---

[9] *Kahler* decision at 21.
[10] Breyer dissent at 17.

use that expression to refer only to whether the defendant intended to act in a certain way.[11]

Breyer's claim that past commentators used language differently than contemporary commentators threatens to undermine his opinion as well as Kagan's. Common law commentary from Bracton to *M'Naghten* was rooted in older notions of lunacy. The very expression, "mental illness" reflects contemporary sensibilities. Lunatics had delusions. Don Quixote confuses windmills with powerful knights. Lunatics do not appreciate the morality or legality of their conduct for the same reason they cannot do complex algebra or even simple arithmetic. They have the intelligence of a small child. The two examples Breyer uses both involve delusions. The accused person thought the victim was a dog or thought the dog ordered the murder. Contemporary psychiatrists do not use the term "lunatic" and do not understand mental illness as the judges did in *M'Naghten*. To understand why we might or might not punish Kahler for his crimes, we need to understand why contemporary psychiatrists think severe depression might induce a person to commit crimes.

Psychiatry

The relationship between "severe depression" and crime is complex. The presence of a diagnosed illness does not explain how the condition may affect the conscious mind in ways relevant to legal decisions: choice, planning, interpretation, and moral judgment. The shared features or criteria for recognizing "severe depression" require the person to experience persistently five of nine criterion symptoms including sad, empty, or otherwise dysphoric mood, and diminished ability to experience or anticipate pleasure.[12] The other criteria include agitation, or slowed movement and thought, or marked disruption of other bodily functions such as sleep, appetite, concentration, and energy. The characteristic state

---

[11]See Alexander Hamilton, James Madison, and John Jay, *The Federalist Papers* (edited by Clinton Rossiter) (New American Library: New York, 1961), page 82; Breyer dissent at 9.

[12]*Diagnostic and Statistical Manual of Mental Disorders*, 5th ed. (2013); World Health Organization, *International Statistical Classification of Diseases and Related Health Problems*, 11th ed. (2020).

of mind of someone who is depressed is one of negative self-assessment, feelings of helplessness or inability to improve one's circumstances, guilt over perceived past failures and transgressions, and despair about the future. Brooding is common. A preoccupation with death, including a wish for one's own death, is another criterion symptom. People may be profoundly anxious or irritable, to a degree that far exceeds the circumstances they may believe justify their feelings. These intense emotions often reflect dysregulation of normal neurological processes modulating elemental fear or rage that originate in the nonconscious brain.

Professional judgment of severity of depression typically connotes the number or degree of symptoms. Severity may also refer to the development of particular psychotic features. So-called "mood congruent" psychosis implies divergence from a normal understanding of reality. The divergence may be perceptual, in the form of hallucinated voices that may be misperceived as coming from outside the person. In depressive psychosis, these voices often accuse the person of crimes or sins, "explaining" their feelings of guilt or badness. They also may counsel despair or hopelessness, as well as suspiciousness of others. Delusions—complex unrealistic beliefs—may also occur in severe depression; the person mistakenly attributes internally generated feelings of guilt, helplessness, or victimization to the actions of others. Such manifestation of severe depression may distort a person's judgment of what is right and wrong. The best studied example of this phenomenon is psychotically depressed mothers who kill children in the false belief that they saving them from some terrible fate.[13]

Understanding how severe depression that includes psychosis may lead a person to criminal conduct is not difficult. Because the mental processes occur outside of awareness, the person misperceives the source of hallucinations or delusions, attributing them to the actions of others to whom they may direct efforts to relieve their torment. The person may still be able to formulate and carry out complex plans, as the illness may spare this capacity, but their distorted thinking motivates behavior that they would not perform if they were not ill.

---

[13]Susan Hatters Friedman and Phillip J. Resnick, "Child Murder by Mothers: Patterns and Prevention," *World Psychiatry* 6, no. 3 (2007): 137–141.

Relating depression without psychosis to criminal conduct is not so straightforward. People in the throes of depression typically overestimate their helplessness and guilt. Because they cannot anticipate pleasure or reward, they view the future as inevitably as painful and empty as the present. Turning this despair into a desire to punish or obliterate those perceived as the cause of their suffering is a possible result of such thinking. Though violence towards others is actually rare in severe depression, initiating violence in the hopes of being killed in return, sometimes called "suicide by cop" does sometimes occur.

Depression may sometimes represent one episode within an even more complex condition: manic depressive or bipolar disorder. People with bipolar disorder may experience both depressive episodes and periods of increased energy, decreased need for sleep, increased goal-directed activity, increased sexual drive, and decreased ability to assess risk, leading to impulsive, risky behavior. People with this condition may develop a mixed state, in which the increased energy and impulsiveness coexist with the negative mood and distorted negative thinking of depression. Such people are at great risk for destructive and self-destructive behavior, associated with catastrophic inability to reason based on the consequences of their actions.

Lunatics and the Mentally Ill in Ancient Law and Contemporary Medicine

The limited evidence suggests that neither *M'Naghten* nor any other long-standing test for insanity capture why Kahler went on a murderous spree on November 28, 2009. Kahler did not think his estranged spouse was a dog or that a deity commanded him to kill family members. The more probable account is that Kahler's marital problems brought about a severe depressive state in which he regarded his life as meaningless and blamed his estranged spouse for his relentless distress. When doing battle over how Blackstone thought about lunatics, neither Kagan nor Breyer said much relevant to how contemporary psychiatrists think about insanity.

Kagan correctly noted that courts are ill-suited to make psychiatric judgments. "Defining the precise relationship between criminal culpability and mental illness," she observed, "involves examining the workings of the brain, the purposes of the criminal law, the ideas of free will and responsibility." Such efforts, she continued, "should be open to revision over time, as new medical knowledge emerges and as legal and moral norms evolve."[14] Jefferson may have had the requisite knowledge. No member of the Roberts Court does.

Kagan's conclusion that revising the insanity defense "is a project for state governance, not constitutional law"[15] is nevertheless problematic. Both the Kagan and Breyer opinions assume that state legislators consider "new medical knowledge" when updating the insanity defense. *M'Naghten's* survival in slightly plus or minus forms across the universe of state law suggests the contrary. *Kahler's* pretenses to the contrary, state legislators have little motivation to change laws designed to excuse lunatics of criminal responsibility in ways that capture what contemporary psychiatrists know and do not know about mental illness. Moreover, the consequences of mental illnesses do not vary by state. Invoking different standards of culpability based upon the location of a crime confounds rational understating of the effects of mental illness upon behavior, criminal or not.

---

[14] *Kahler* decision, page 24.
[15] Ibid.

9

Kelly v. US on Public Fraud and the Bridgegate Controversy

Jennifer Bowie

In 2015, Bridget Anne Kelly and her co-conspirator William Baroni were convicted on federal fraud charges because of a plot they hatched and carried out against the Mayor of Fort Lee, New Jersey—an act of political revenge that became known as "Bridgegate." The Bridgegate controversy contains all the hallmarks of a political thriller: wrongdoing, fraud, deception, corruption, political payback, cover-ups, traffic jams, and a bridge. Watergate, Spygate, Deflategate… Bridgegate is only the latest in the line of "gate" scandals; however, the conduct at issue in Bridgegate reverberated not only in the social and political consciousness, but also in the hallways of the US Supreme Court.

J. Bowie (✉)
University of Richmond, Richmond, VA, USA

© The Author(s) 2021
M. Marietta (ed.), *SCOTUS 2020*,
https://doi.org/10.1007/978-3-030-53851-4_9

The Scandal

The story begins with the George Washington Bridge, dubbed the "busiest bridge in the world," which connects Fort Lee and Manhattan.[1] The bridge is operated by the Port Authority of New York and New Jersey, a bi-state agency. On the upper level of the double-decker suspension bridge are twelve toll lanes that direct traffic from New Jersey to Manhattan. Under a decades-old agreement between New Jersey and Fort Lee, the Port Authority reserves three of the twelve George Washington Bridge lanes for Fort Lee local access (known as "Special Access Lanes") during morning rush hour. The other nine lanes (known as "Main Line Lanes") are open to all traffic from Interstates 80 and 95.

The scandal started in 2013 during then-New Jersey Governor Chris Christie's reelection campaign. As part of his reelection strategy, Christie wanted broad bipartisan support within his state from local leaders because he had his eyes set on running for President of the United States. Part of Christie's bipartisan strategy included courting Democratic leaders, particularly mayors, for endorsements. Christie's Chief of Staff, Bridget Anne Kelly, managed relations with these local leaders. When Kelly approached the mayor of Fort Lee, Mark Sokolich, seeking campaign support, Sokolich informed Kelly that he would not back Christie's reelection effort.

After learning of Sokolich's perceived disloyalty, Kelly set upon a course of retribution. Kelly personally contacted the Port Authority Deputy Executive Director, William Baroni, and another Port Authority official, David Wildstein—both of whom were appointed by Christie. The trio brainstormed ideas to punish the mayor. Wildstein proposed to open the three dedicated Fort Lee Special Access Lanes to all traffic, which would cause debilitating rush hour gridlock on the local streets of Fort Lee. Kelly readily agreed to the idea and memorialized her approval of the scheme in an email in which she wrote: "Time for some traffic problems in Fort Lee."[2]

---

[1] www.panynj.gov/bridges-tunnels/en/george-washington-bridge.html.
[2] *Kelly* decision, page 3.

However, in order to carry out the lane change plot, Wildstein needed to create a "legitimate" cover story since he did not have unilateral authority to make this lane change policy himself and he knew the Director of the Port Authority, Patrick Foye, would never agree to make such a change based upon their true motivation, political payback. The cover story concocted went something like this: the Port Authority would conduct a "traffic study" in order to determine whether the Special Access Lanes should remain in effect. To make the story plausible, Wildstein directed Port Authority employees to collect data on the resulting traffic and delays. But this so-called traffic study "bore little resemblance to the Port Authority's usual traffic studies," and as one of the engineers testified, the Port Authority "never closes lanes to study traffic patterns" since computer models can effectively "predict the effect of such actions."[3]

There was one small setback to Wildstein's story; the Port Authority's head engineer informed the three that if they opened the Special Access Lanes to everyone the likelihood of side swipe crashes would dramatically increase. As a compromise Wildstein agreed to leave one Special Access Lane open to Fort Lee commuters. This required the Port Authority to hire additional toll collectors to man the Special Access Lane. Why? Normally when Fort Lee toll collectors need a break they simply close their lane and drivers use one of the other two Special Access Lanes. However, under this new one-lane plan, an additional toll collector had to be "on call" to fill in.

On the morning of September 9, 2013, the Port Authority employees—without warning to Fort Lee officials—implemented the scheme and adjusted the dedicated Special Access Lanes from three down to one. Unsurprisingly, the Fort Lee morning rush hour traffic came to a screeching halt and "rivaled that of 9/11 when the George Washington Bridge shutdown."[4] The Special Access Lane closures were not just a nuisance for Fort Lee residents but also dangerous; school buses were stuck on the streets for hours, ambulances faced immense difficulties in

---

[3]Ibid. at 4.
[4]Ibid. at 5.

responding to emergencies, and the police "had trouble responding to a report of a missing child."[5] In short, it was chaos.

The mayor of Fort Lee made several calls to the Port Authority, including Baroni, all of which were ignored—including text messages. The Access Lane closures went on for three additional days and were stopped only when Executive Director Foye found out and unilaterally reversed the lane closure decision. The fallout was swift; not only did Kelly, Baroni, and Wildstein lose their jobs, they were also criminally charged with violating federal wire fraud statutes.

The Trial and Appeal to the Third Circuit

Under federal fraud laws it is a crime to effect "any scheme or artifice to defraud, or for obtaining money or property by means of false or fraudulent pretenses, representations, or promises" with the use of the wires.[6] In other words, federal fraud laws prohibit deceptive schemes that deprive entities of money or property. This means that the government must prove both deception and that the *intent* of the fraud was to obtain money or property. Under the government's theory, the victim of the cover-up was the Port Authority, because Kelly and Baroni had fraudulently deprived the Port Authority of property (the taking over the Special Access Lanes) and money (the cost in salary to carry out the fake traffic study), for political retribution.[7]

The Court makes clear in the decision that public officials only violate the law when their deception is for "obtaining money or property."[8] These requirements prevent the government from criminalizing merely "dishonest acts by state and local officials."[9] Suppose a local councilman uses deception to get city employees to landscape his yard. Or suppose a mayor has her private driveway plowed by city employees, or a city

---

[5] Ibid.
[6] 18 U.S.C §1343.
[7] *U.S. v. Baroni*, 909 F.3d 550 (3d Cir, 2018), page 561.
[8] *Kelly* decision, page 7.
[9] Ibid.

worker is tricked into painting the Governor's beach home. In these examples the point of the deception is to acquire public resources for a private benefit. But did "commandeering" two Special Access Lanes under the guise of a traffic study, for which engineers and toll booth workers were paid, count as obtaining money or property within the purview of the statute? Federal prosecutors, the jury, and, later, the US Circuit Court of Appeals for the Third Circuit thought so.

Almost two years after Kelly and Baroni were fired and after an over year-long investigation, a federal grand jury indicted them on seven counts of wire fraud. Wildstein ultimately pled guilty to two counts in return for his cooperation. At trial, the prosecution showed the jury that the defendants used property—the Special Access Lanes and toll booths—to purposely create a traffic jam. Wildstein testified that he "agreed to change the lane configuration for purposes of causing – punishing Mark Sokolich, of creating a traffic jam that would punish him, send him a message" because the Mayor of Fort Lee had not endorsed Governor Christie.[10] Additionally, the prosecution further showed that the salaries from overtime toll workers and Port Authority professional staff to carry out the scheme was tantamount to obtaining property: "the salary paid to overtime toll booth collectors for the one remaining toll booth that was accessible to Fort Lee, the money paid to Baroni and Wildstein themselves while they were wasting their time in furtherance of this conspiracy and money paid to the engineers who wasted time and Port Authority professional staff, who wasted time collecting data that no one ever wanted."[11] The prosecution in their case in chief also noted that the cover story was a key component to their scheme. In order to carry out their plan, Kelly and Baroni had to come up with the traffic study cover because Baroni did not have unilateral regulatory authority to change the Special Access Lanes Fort Lee received. In other words, as the prosecution viewed it, if he had to lie about what was going on, he was not authorized to alter the Special Access Lanes. This suggested to the jury that the political payback plan should not be

---

[10] *U.S. v. Baroni*, 909 F.3d 550 (3d Cir, 2018), page 557.
[11] Ibid. at 561.

chalked up to Baroni's claim that it fit under his normal authority for regulatory decision-making.

On the other hand, Kelly and Baroni suggested at trial that their actions were merely a reallocation of public resources and the motive for the realignment does not matter under federal fraud statutes (even if the public official concealed the true motive) because the object of their plan was not to obtain property or money. They further suggested that they did not "deprive the Port Authority of any tangible property" because the Port Authority still owned the toll booth and lanes and the public had access to them.[12] Ultimately, the jury convicted Kelly and Baroni, and the trial court sentenced both to 18 months in federal prison (Kelly's sentence was ultimately reduced to 13 months).

On appeal, the Third Circuit Court of Appeals upheld the criminal convictions. The three-judge panel unanimously agreed with the government's showing that the requirements of the fraud statute had been met. In fact, for the Third Circuit the fraud violation was clear: Kelly and Baroni deceived Port Authority officials when they lied about the need for a traffic study to justify closing two of the three Special Access Lanes. The Third Circuit reasoned that their deception deprived the Port Authority of its property in two ways: (1) its right to control the bridge lanes and (2) the cost of unnecessary labor (it cost approximately $5400 in labor costs for the on-call toll collectors and the traffic engineers to conduct the fake traffic study). In the panel's view these lies and deception deprived the Port Authority of both tangible (the bridge lanes) and intangible (the salary costs) property for political payback. Kelly and Baroni appealed their case to the US Supreme Court.

Kelly at the Court

The key question for the Court was whether Kelly and Baroni committed property fraud. During oral arguments, the appellants claimed that even though their behavior was an abuse of power, their scheme should not be characterized as trying to obtain money or property. Instead it was

---

[12]Ibid. at 562.

a regulatory decision in how the bridge lanes were allocated. In other words, while it was wrong for the two to lie, their motive for the lie did not matter because their deception was not to obtain money or property. Conversely the government argued that Kelly and Baroni violated federal fraud statutes when they told the lie and commandeered the Special Access Lanes—"by taking control of its physical lanes"—for political payback.[13] The government argued the cover-up was essential to their plan, because without the so-called traffic study, the lanes could not be reallocated from the Special Access Lanes to the Main Line Lanes by Baroni and Kelly, because they did not have the unilateral authority to do so. In the end, the Court was unmoved by the government's arguments.

In the unanimous opinion, Justice Elena Kagan, writing for the Court, threw out the convictions. She noted in her questioning during the oral arguments that the object of the scheme was to create a traffic jam, not to obtain property. Kagan made clear in the ruling that "save for bribes or kickback (not at issue here), a state or local official's fraudulent schemes violate the law only when, again, they are for 'obtaining money or property.'"[14] The Court could not accept the government or lower court's argument that when the Special Access Lanes were reallocated to the Main Line Lanes, this was tantamount to "obtaining property" and that the schemers deprived the Port Authority of the costs to fund the compensation of the toll booth operators and traffic engineers.[15] Moreover, the Court did not believe the objective of the cover-up was to take Port Authority property. In their view the objective of the scheme was clearly to create a traffic jam.

The Court insisted that the government did not prove that Kelly and Baroni's fraudulent plan was directed at obtaining property and money from the Port Authority. The property, in their view, was just the cost of doing business, or as the Court put it, a "run-of-the-mine exercise of regulatory power."[16] While the government and lower court saw Kelly and Baroni's actions as commandeering bridge lanes, the Court saw it as

---

[13] *Kelly* decision, page 8.
[14] Ibid. at 7.
[15] Ibid. at 8.
[16] Ibid. at 10.

merely exercising regulatory choice in appropriating government property. Kagan pointed out that Baroni and Kelly "did not walk away with the lanes; nor did they take the lanes from the Government by converting them to non-public use," instead she argued that they "regulated use of lanes, as officials responsible for roadways often do."[17] For the Court, although the Special Access Lane reconfiguration occurred under false pretenses the object of their fraud was not to take property. In other words, Kelly and Baroni did not, in the literal sense, take property by depriving access to the lanes for nonpublic use when exercising this regulatory authority (recall, when the lanes were realigned from the Special Access Lanes to the Main Line Lanes the public still had access to the lanes).

How did the Court address the cost of labor employed for the faux traffic study? As the Government argued, the work of the engineers was crucial to carrying out the cover-up since Baroni (or Wildstein) did not have the authority to realign the lanes unilaterally. The Court disagreed. In addressing the labor costs to carry out the plan the Court reasoned that the cost of compensation was an "incidental by product" of the scheme. The Court argued that the toll collectors, for example, just had to "sit there and wait," and they did no personal work for Baroni or Kelly. The Court also pointed out that but for the Chief Engineer restoring one of the Special Access Lanes to Fort Lee, the original plan hatched by the appellants did not call for extra toll collectors. This provided additional support for the Court's view that the objective of the appellants was not to obtain employee labor; it was to close all of the Special Access Lanes to create a massive traffic jam in Fort Lee to punish the mayor for failing to support Christie's reelection bid. The Court noted that "every regulatory decision requires the use of some employee labor. But that doesn't mean every scheme to alter a regulation has that labor as its object."[18]

This is not the first time the Court has reined in the use of federal fraud and corruption statutes by prosecutors to criminalize state and local behavior. The Court in a series of cases—*McNally v. United States* (1987), *Cleveland v. United States* (2000), *Skilling v. United States*

---

[17]Ibid. at 9.
[18]Ibid. at 12, 11, and 12.

(2010), and *McDonald v. United States* (2016)—has ruled that prosecutors may not use the criminal laws to target behavior or policies it finds unsavory. As the Court argued in *Kelly*, if these limits where not in place federal power would balloon and "in effect, the Federal Government could use the criminal law to enforce (its view of) integrity in broad swaths of state and local policymaking."[19] For the current Court, the statutory interpretation of federal fraud and corruption statutes is a matter of exactly what the law says. Under our system of law, prosecutors may want to extend the bounds of criminal behavior—even for the good cause of fighting corruption—but they cannot until the legislature authorizes them to do so, and the Court makes this clear in the *Kelly* case.

Conclusion

The *Kelly* decision reveals a clear pattern of the Court's willingness to push back against using federal fraud statues to fight public corruption. At the end of the day, the Court viewed Kelly and Baroni's abuse of power as wrong, corrupt, and deceptive, but not criminal under federal fraud statutes. The Court likened their behavior to ordinary regulatory decision-making even if their motive was political payback. What Kelly and Baroni wanted to do was create a traffic jam in Fort Lee; their scheme and deception was not about not obtaining property (the lanes) or money (the employee labor). The Court in the *Kelly* decision once again reigns in how far prosecutors can go in applying federal fraud statutes to fight corruption.

---

[19]Ibid. at 12.

10

Mcgirt v. Oklahoma on Native Rights

Carol Nackenoff and Natasha Markov-Riss

What began as an unusual argument by the defense in a criminal prosecution became a major controversy about the existence of an Indian reservation in a large part of the state of Oklahoma. Patrick Dwayne Murphy and Jimcy McGirt are unsympathetic felons, one convicted of a horrific murder and the other of a child rape. The grounds for their appeals, however, concern their status as Native Americans: Their crimes took place on land that was once a reservation established by the federal government, yet their prosecutions were conducted by state authorities under the belief that the reservation ceased to exist over 100 years ago. *McGirt v. Oklahoma* addresses the controversies over tribal sovereignty and the historical mistreatment of Native Americans, with implications for former tribal lands and Native sovereignty in other parts of the United States.

C. Nackenoff (✉) · N. Markov-Riss
Swarthmore College, Swarthmore, PA, USA

© The Author(s) 2021   111
M. Marietta (ed.), *SCOTUS 2020*,
https://doi.org/10.1007/978-3-030-53851-4_10

Reservations, Please

The specific issue presented in *McGirt* was whether the 1885 Major Crimes Act—which established federal authority over a number of crimes committed by Native Americans against each other on tribal lands—precludes the State of Oklahoma from prosecuting such crimes in its state courts. The question is complicated by the long history of relations between the federal government and the Native tribes, as well as the confusing relationship between the federal government and states in many arenas of Native American governance. At issue in *McGirt*, as well as in an almost identical case heard but not decided the previous term, was the question of whether the 1866 territorial boundaries of the Creek Nation constitute an "Indian reservation." If so, had Congress *disestablished* the reservation or not?

The Supreme Court seemed poised to settle the issue in 2018 when it chose to hear *Sharp v. Murphy*.[1] In 2000, the Oklahoma state court convicted Murphy of the murder of a fellow Creek Nation member, sentencing him to death. Murphy appealed on the grounds that Oklahoma lacked jurisdiction under the Major Crimes Act (MCA): his crime should have been tried in federal court. The state court and Oklahoma's Court of Criminal Appeals rejected his argument. Upon appeal in federal district court, Murphy again lost: the 1866 territorial boundaries did not constitute a reservation, preserving Oklahoma's jurisdiction. However, when the case went to the Tenth Circuit (the highest federal Court of Appeal before reaching the Supreme Court) the federal judges reversed this decision, taking the opposite position on the existence of a reservation:

All land within the borders of an Indian reservation—regardless of whether the tribe, individual Indians, or non-Indians hold title to a given tract of land—is Indian country unless Congress has disestablished the reservation or diminished its borders… Applying the Supreme

---

[1] *Sharp v. Murphy*, previously known as *Royal v. Murphy*, and then *Carpenter v. Murphy*, reflected the names of successive prison wardens and interim wardens. Murphy's victim was George Jacobs, also Creek, to whom his girlfriend had previously been married.

Court's test to determine whether Congress has done so as to the Creek Reservation, we conclude it has not.[2]

The case was argued in the Supreme Court in November 2018, but Justice Gorsuch recused himself due to previous involvement in the case as a federal appellate judge. The remaining Justices were unable to reach a decision. They placed the case on the calendar for reargument in the October 2019 term.

With *Sharp v. Murphy* still in limbo, a 71-year-old member of the Muscogee (Creek) Nation, Jimcy McGirt, filed an *in forma pauperis* petition from prison, and the Supreme Court—surprising even Indian law experts—granted him a hearing.[3] Upon McGirt's request, the Court appointed Ian Gershengorn (former Acting Solicitor General of the United States under President Obama and prominent advocate of Native rights) as his counsel of record. A tiny percentage of the many *in forma pauperis* petitions filed are accepted by the Court, yet when these cases are heard, they sometimes result in very important decisions, as in *Gideon v. Wainwright* (1961), the case establishing the right to counsel for poor defendants in criminal trials.

McGirt, a member of the Seminole Nation, had been convicted after a jury trial—in an Oklahoma state court—of rape, sodomy, and other sex crimes against a four-year-old Seminole girl on the Creek reservation. He was sentenced to serve two consecutive 500-year terms with no opportunity of parole. The Court of Criminal Appeals upheld McGirt's conviction, affirming Oklahoma's jurisdiction to prosecute his crimes. McGirt appealed directly to the Supreme Court.

In both *Sharp* and *McGirt*, the Trump Administration sided with Oklahoma, arguing that Congress intended to disestablish the Creek Nation's reservation when it created the State of Oklahoma. The brief for the United States pointed out that, for over a century, the United States and Oklahoma have operated with that understanding.

Concerns about recognition of the reservation included the unraveling of long-term practices and the administrative nightmares likely to

---

[2] *Murphy v. Royal* 866 F.3d 1164, 1171–1172 (10th Cir., 2017).

[3] An *in forma pauperis* petition (from Latin, "in the manner of a pauper") allows a party with no financial resources, often a prisoner, to file without the usual fees.

ensue. "The overwhelming majority of Tulsa's landmass and population lies within the former territory of the Creek and Cherokee Nations," a brief by the City of Tulsa states. Should the Court declare all of this reservation land, "nearly 95% of Tulsa's land and over 98% of its population would suddenly find themselves in the jurisdictional and regulatory morass that is 'Indian country'."[4]

Justice Neil Gorsuch seemed poised to play a pivotal role in *McGirt*. While serving on the 10th Circuit, Judge Gorsuch, a Westerner, had often expressed the importance of honoring treaty obligations and other statutory commitments the federal government had made with Native Americans. This comports with his public commitment to textualism, including the view that specific language employed by Congress is binding until explicitly altered. Gorsuch would not only be decisive to the outcome but would write the majority opinion in *McGirt*.

Historical Background

The Muscogee Creek, Chickasaw, Cherokee, Choctaw, and Seminole tribes were forcibly removed from their homelands in the eastern United States in the 1830s, suffering terrible human losses on the Trail of Tears. The Indian Removal Act of 1830 authorized President Andrew Jackson to grant Native Americans federal land west of the Mississippi in exchange for their lands within eastern state borders. Though some, including the Creek, resisted, they were forced to leave for the reservations granted to them. By the 1832 treaty, the Creeks were promised that "[no] State or Territory [shall] ever have a right to pass laws for the government of such Indians, but they shall be allowed to govern themselves."[5]

Following the Civil War, these tribes were divested of the western half of the federally issued lands on the grounds that some had allied with and supported the Confederacy. The remaining lands—roughly 19

---

[4]Brief of the City of Tulsa as Amicus Curiae in Support of Respondent (Oklahoma), pages 1, 28.
[5]1832 Treaty with the Creeks, Art. XIV, 7 Stat. 368, quoted in *McGirt* decision page 1.

million acres constituting much of Eastern Oklahoma—were retained and governed by these tribes. They became known as the Five Civilized Tribes because they established constitutional governments and tended to adopt Christianity and western dress.

The Major Crimes Act, the core law at issue here, was passed by Congress following public outcry over *Ex parte Crow Dog* (1883), in which a murder committed by one tribal member against another was held unreachable by Dakota territorial courts, leaving only a lenient tribal court sentence. The new Act established federal jurisdiction over serious crimes committed on Native American reservations, including murder, manslaughter, kidnapping, incest, assault against an individual under age 16, felony child abuse, rape, burglary, and robbery.[6]

In 1887, Congress passed the General Allotment Act (Dawes Act), designed to expedite the division of reservations into individual plots and encourage each family to live separately. The "surplus" land not allocated would be held in trust by the federal government, and much of it was "freed up" for sale to white settlers.[7] While the Dawes Act included a 25-year period of tutelage during which the new Native American owners could not sell their land or be duped into parting with it by unscrupulous whites, many whites eventually came to own lands among Native Americans, including formerly allotted land.

In 1893, Senator Henry Dawes headed a commission to the Five Civilized Tribes, trying to get them to participate in allotment of their lands, but they resisted. Dawes emphasized that Congress had the power to enforce allotment, and that they would be better off participating in allotment decisions. In 1897, Dawes reached an agreement with the Creek. They would receive 160-acre allotments and the government would sell the surplus lands, with proceeds benefitting the Creeks. One of the Oklahoma's core arguments in *McGirt* was that allotment of individually owned parcels of land to Creek Nation members and subsequent

---

[6]See S. Lee Martin, "Indian Rights and the Constitutional Implications of the Major Crimes Act," *Notre Dame Law Review* 52 (1976): 109–135.

[7]Carol Nackenoff, "Constitutionalizing Terms of Inclusion: Friends of the Indian and Citizenship for Native Americans, 1880s–1930s," in *The Supreme Court and American Political Development*, eds. Ronald Kahn and Ken I. Kersch (Lawrence: University Press of Kansas, 2006): 366–413.

sale of surplus land intentionally (if subtly) ended the existence of the reservation.

Also relevant to McGirt's case was a long history of Supreme Court holdings that the federal government, not the states, exercised sole jurisdiction over Native American tribes.[8] The Court eventually held that Congress could abrogate treaties and diminish or eliminate reservations unilaterally.[9] But had Congress clearly and intentionally ended the treaty obligations with the Creek Nation and disestablished the reservation?

The Majority Opinion

"On the far end of the Trail of Tears was a promise," Gorsuch begins. Does the land promised to the Creek Nation in 1830 remain an Indian reservation? Gorsuch concludes that "[b]ecause Congress has not said otherwise, we hold the government to its word."[10]

The Indian Removal Act was meant "to assure the tribe... that the United States will forever secure and guaranty to them... the country so exchanged with them." In an 1856 treaty, Congress promised that "no portion" of the Creek Reservation "shall ever be embraced or included within, or annexed to, any Territory or State."[11] "Under any definition," Gorsuch writes, "this was a reservation."[12]

The majority rejected what they termed Oklahoma's "hodge-podge" of arguments. First, allotment of land cannot be equated to cession: The Court pointed to precedents holding that Congress does not disestablish a reservation when it allows the transfer of individual plots, whether

---

[8] See *Worcester v. Georgia*, 31 U.S. 515 (1832), the final case in what is known as the "Marshall Trilogy" (referring to Chief Justice John Marshall), in which the Court recognized the independent standing of the Indian Nations. If Native Americans left their tribes and assimilated, they were presumably subject to state jurisdiction; this issue became more confusing during the allotment era.

[9] See *Lone Wolf v. Hitchcock*, 187 U.S. 553 (1903), frequently referred to as the Native Americans' *Dred Scott*; *Solem v. Bartlett*, 465 U.S. 463 (1984); *South Dakota v. Yankton Sioux Tribe*, 522 U.S. 329 (1998).

[10] *McGirt* decision, page 1.

[11] Indian Removal Act of 1830, §3, 4 Stat. 412; Ratified Treaty No. 303 (August 7, 1856) with the Creek and Seminole Indians, Art. 4, 11 Stat. 700.

[12] *McGirt* decision, pages 4–6.

to Native Americans or others.[13] Congress may have passed allotment laws to create the *conditions* for disestablishment, but "wishes are not laws" and "future plans aren't either." After allotment, the tribe retained "significant sovereign functions over the lands in question."[14] Referencing another major precedent, *Nebraska v. Parker* (2016), the majority insisted there must be clear evidence of express congressional intent to disestablish the reservation, often with "[e]xplicit reference to cession or other language evidencing the present and total surrender of all tribal interests."[15]

Goruch's opinion challenged Oklahoma's interpretation of the test for congressional diminishment of a reservation set out in *Solem v. Bartlett* (1984). *Solem* stipulated that "[t]he effect of any given surplus land Act depends on the language of the Act and the circumstances underlying its passage."[16] Oklahoma claimed *Solem* required three distinct steps: an examination of the laws passed by Congress, then of the relevant context, and then subsequent understandings of the text. The majority held that the "only 'step' proper for a court of law... is to ascertain and follow the original meaning of the law before us." In short, "there is no need to consult extra-textual sources when the meaning of a statute's terms is clear."[17] The majority found no ambiguous language.

Ultimately, the opinion ends where it began, with the sanctity of Congress' promise to the Creek Nation. "If Congress wishes to withdraw its promises, it must say so." Inconvenience is no reason to disregard text, and "unlawful acts, performed long enough and with sufficient vigor, are never enough to amend the law." The opinion recognized that the consequences of the Court's ruling are "not insignificant," but "the magnitude of a legal wrong is no reason to perpetuate it."[18]

---

[13] See *Mattz v. Arnett*, 412 U.S. 463 (1973) at 497 ("[A]llotment under the ... Act is completely consistent with continued reservation status").

[14] *McGirt* decision, pages 12, 14.

[15] Ibid. at 8, quoting *Nebraska v. Parker*, 577 U.S. 481, ___ (2016).

[16] *Solem v. Bartlett*, 465 U.S. 463 (1984) at 469.

[17] *McGirt* decision, pages 18, 20.

[18] Ibid. at 3, 38, and 42. The Court decided *Sharp v. Murphy* the same day, issuing a per curiam opinion affirming the 10th Circuit ruling in light of the decision in *McGirt*.

The Dissenters

Chief Justice Roberts—in the majority in all but one other case decided this term—wrote the dissenting opinion, joined by Justices Alito, Kavanaugh, and Thomas.[19] The dissenters agreed with Oklahoma that, following the precedents of *Solem* and *Parker*, the text is not the only consideration in determining disestablishment; surrounding circumstances and "subsequent understanding of the status of the reservation and the pattern of settlement there" matter.[20] Roberts points to the purpose of allotment; the grant of US citizenship to members of the Creek Nation shortly thereafter; Acts of Congress leading up to statehood and the way those acts were understood both by the Dawes Commission and the Creeks at the time of their passage; the several mentions in the US Code of "former Indian reservations"; and the fact that "for 113 years, Oklahoma has asserted jurisdiction over the former Indian Territory on the understanding that it is not a reservation, without any objection from the Five Tribes until recently," as conclusive evidence of congressional intent.[21] In Roberts' view, interpreting the Congress' purpose as anything other than disestablishment of the reservation is "fantasy" given that "through an open and concerted effort, Congress did what it set out to do: transform a reservation into a State."[22]

The dissenters were also quite disturbed by the possible adverse consequences of the decision, which "may destabilize the governance of vast swathes of Oklahoma."[23] They fear that decades of past convictions could be thrown out. Oklahoma's ability to prosecute serious crimes involving Native Americans on reservations in eastern Oklahoma will now be seriously hobbled. Reservation status adds confusion to many areas of law by conferring "tribal government power over numerous areas

---

[19]Roberts joined a dissent in *Ramos v. Louisiana* against the majority holding that the Sixth Amendment required a unanimous guilty verdict from juries in state criminal trials (see Chapter 12).

[20]Roberts dissent at 6, citing *Solem v. Bartlett*, 465 U.S. 463, 470–472 (1984).

[21]Ibid. at 31–32.

[22]Ibid. at 22–23.

[23]Ibid. at 1.

Fig. 10.1 The 1866 territories of the "Five Civilized Tribes" in Oklahoma (Scholastic Inc./Jim McMahon)

of life—including powers over non-Indian citizens and businesses." The consequences are, in short, "drastic"[24] (Fig. 10.1).

Significance

The decision strongly implies that there are four additional reservations in eastern Oklahoma aside from the Creek's, and with Native Americans comprising 10–15% of the 1.8 million residents living in eastern Oklahoma, there are bound to be important repercussions. Lawyers will have to explore what aspects of civil procedure, taxation, business regulation, and policing may be unsettled by *Mcgirt*. Jimcy McGirt, Patrick Dwayne Murphy, and many others convicted of criminal offenses in state court are likely to be retried in federal court. Oklahoma stands to lose its ability to prosecute Indians for crimes committed in most of the city of Tulsa. It is uncertain that federal jurisdiction will do anything to address

---

[24]Ibid. at 36, 37.

Native American complaints that rates of incarceration, police violence, treatment of juvenile offenders, and the criminal justice system in general discriminate against them.[25]

The Principal Chief of the Creek Nation, David Hill, said "This is a historic day... This is amazing. It's never too late to make things right." Surprised that the federal government kept its promises to Native Americans, tribes began to imagine a new chapter in relations between themselves and federal courts. The chief counsel for Jimcy McGirt said: "The Supreme Court reaffirmed today that when the United States makes promises, the courts will keep those promises. Congress persuaded the Creek Nation to walk the Trail of Tears with promises of a reservation—and the Court today correctly recognized that this reservation endures."[26]

Yet the US government does not want to have to try all cases covered by the MCA in federal court, and some crimes may go unprosecuted. Congress could address this problem by stating clearly that it was disestablishing the reservation or by granting Oklahoma authority to try major crimes, using the language of cession. However, given the late twentieth-century movement toward restoring tribal self-governance, this might be politically unpalatable.

In a joint statement after the ruling, leaders of the Muscogee Creek, Cherokee, Chickasaw, Choctaw, and Seminole Nations and the State of Oklahoma announced they were close to an agreement for proposed federal legislation that would resolve the jurisdictional issues raised by the case. A plan announced by Oklahoma's Attorney General a week later did not gain assent from leaders of the Creek and Seminole Nations.[27]

McGirt looks, for the moment, like a major victory for Native Americans, especially those of eastern Oklahoma, and suggests that the textualist approach of Justice Gorsuch may hold additional promise for them.

---

[25] See, for example, Lakota People's Law Project, Native Lives Matter (February 2015).

[26] Chris Polansky, Public Radio Tulsa (10 July 2020), quoting Ian Gershengorn.

[27] Sean Murray, "Two Tribal Leaders Say They Don't Support Agreement," Associated Press (17 July 2020).

11

New York State Rifle & Pistol v. City of New York on Gun Regulation

Austin Sarat

2008 brought an abrupt turnaround in Second Amendment jurisprudence when the Supreme Court handed down its *District of Columbia
v. Heller* ruling.[1] For most of the Court's history, it said little about the
Second Amendment, and, when it did, found that the right to bear arms
applied to militias and weapons for military service. In *Heller*, Justice
Scalia changed all that.

Writing for a five-judge majority, he struck down a city ordinance
forbidding the private ownership of handguns. He argued that the
Second Amendment protected the right of individuals to possess a
firearm "unconnected with service in a militia, and to use that arm for
traditionally lawful purposes, such as self-defense within the home." But
he also conceded that, like other rights, this right was "not unlimited."[2]

---

[1] See Dan M. Peterson and Stephen P. Halbrook, "A Revolution in Second Amendment Law,"
Widener Law School Delaware University Law Review 29 (2011/2012): 12, 13.
[2] *District of Columbia v. Heller*, 554 U.S. 570 (2008) at 587.

A. Sarat (✉)
Amherst College, Amherst, MA, USA

© The Author(s) 2021
M. Marietta (ed.), *SCOTUS 2020*,
https://doi.org/10.1007/978-3-030-53851-4_11

121

The Court followed up *Heller* two years later when it decided that the Fourteenth Amendment's Due Process Clause incorporates the Second Amendment right and applies it to the states.[3] Yet the sweeping rhetoric of those two cases masked the reality that at the time they were decided only Chicago and Washington, D.C.—but no states—had laws prohibiting handgun possession. Instead of bans, most local governments had a range of restrictions and qualifications to gun ownership and use, which left open the questions of which kinds of limitations on gun rights were constitutionally permissible under *Heller*.

Since then mass shootings have become a regular occurrence in the United States.[4] In response, states and cities have enacted many gun-control measures, including universal background checks, assault-weapons bans, and restrictions on high-capacity magazines.

Yet the Court remained silent about *Heller's* meaning.[5] It left to the lower courts the task of discerning permissible restrictions and scrutinizing particular gun regulations. Over the last decade, those courts have taken different approaches to the threshold question of what standard of review should be employed in Second Amendment cases and reached different conclusions about the constitutionality of particular gun regulations. In the great majority of those cases courts have upheld the challenged gun regulation.[6]

When the Court granted certiorari in *New York State Rifle & Pistol Association, Inc. v. City of New York* (NYSRPA), it seemed poised to make a major ruling clarifying the scope of Second Amendment rights as well as the appropriate standard of review in gun cases. The case involved a challenge to an ordinance restricting licensed gun owners from carrying their weapons outside of their home. Under the City regulation, it was a criminal offense to transport a firearm to any location other than seven designated shooting ranges, which excluded second homes or firing ranges outside the City.

---

[3] *McDonald v. Chicago*, 561 U.S. 742 (2010).
[4] Gun Violence Archive, found at https://www.gunviolencearchive.org/reports/mass-shooting.
[5] Emma Long, "Why So Silent? The Supreme Court and the Second Amendment Debate After *DC v. Heller*," *European Journal of American Studies* 12 (2017).
[6] Eric Ruben and Joseph Blocher, "From Theory to Doctrine: An Empirical Analysis of the Right to Keep and Bear Arms After *Heller*," *Duke Law Journal* 67 (2019): 1433.

"The Passive Virtues"

Although both a federal district court and the Second Circuit Court of Appeals upheld the ban,[7] in June 2019 the City repealed its law. It feared that the litigation would give the Supreme Court a vehicle to craft a further major expansion of gun rights.[8] The Court granted cert anyway. Much of the subsequent argument in the case focused on the question of whether the ordinance's repeal rendered the case moot.

Mootness is one of the most important of what Yale law professor Alexander Bickel once called "the passive virtues."[9] Noting that Supreme Court Justices are appointed rather than elected, Bickel argued that they should interfere as little as possible in the democratic political process, jealously guarding the Court's legitimacy in the face of what he labeled a "countermajoritarian difficulty." He urged judges to avoid involving themselves in political questions by invoking doctrines like mootness.

The idea that courts should refuse to decide moot cases is traced to the common law and the constitutional limitation of judicial power to the resolution of "cases and controversies."[10] Traditionally cases have been found to be moot because the parties settled their dispute or because a law being challenged was repealed or changed.[11]

The gun owners maintained that despite the repeal of the ordinance, a live controversy still existed about whether the City could arrest a licensed gun owner who stops in transit to a legal destination. (The attorney for the City asserted in oral arguments that no arrests would be made for coffee or bathroom stops, but the ordinance as written leaves this in question.) The petitioners urged the Court to bar the City (or any other city) from enforcing a similar ban in the future and also prohibit

---

[7]See *New York State Rifle & Pistol Association v. City of New York*, 86 F. Supp. 3d 249 (S.D.N.Y. 2015) and *New York State Rifle & Pistol Association v. City of New York*, 883 F.3d 45 (2d Cir. 2018).

[8]Richard Wolf, "New York City Limits on Transporting Guns Eased in Effort to Get Supreme Court Challenge Dismissed," *USA Today* (21 June 2019).

[9]Alexander Bickel, "Foreword: The Passive Virtues," *Harvard Law Review* 75 (1960–61): 40.

[10]See *Mills v. Green* 159 U.S. 651, 653 (1895).

[11]Note, "Mootness on Appeal in the Supreme Court," *Harvard Law Review* 83 (1970): 1672.

it from considering past violations of the law in future licensing decisions. The litigants also raised the possibility that they would seek money
as compensation for the violation of their Second Amendment rights.
Moreover, allowing a party to moot a case after the Supreme Court grants
review, they argued, would set a bad precedent that allows local governments to enact unconstitutional restrictions for a number of years only
to repeal them without consequence before the Court rules.

New York City contended that the case was indeed moot because the
gun owners have gotten everything they asked for originally. Governments, it suggested, should be encouraged to end litigation by resolving
matters through the democratic process. In this sense, the repeal was a
victory for constitutionalism rather than a defeat of the system.

In a controversial amicus brief supporting the City's position on the
question of mootness, five Democratic senators led by Sheldon Whitehouse of Rhode Island offered a broad and unprecedented indictment
of the Court's conservative majority.[12] It accused them of pursuing a
"political project" and being in league with the National Rifle Association and other pro-gun groups seeking to radically expand gun owners'
protections provided by the Second Amendment.

Their brief was particularly hard on Justice Kavanaugh, whose confirmation was aggressively pursued by the National Rifle Association. It
quoted an NRA ad supporting Kavanaugh's confirmation: "Four liberal
Justices oppose your right to self-defense... Four Justices support your
right to self-defense. President Trump chose Brett Kavanaugh to break
the tie. Your right to self-defense depends on this vote."

The Court Decides

Instead of making the sweeping decision gun rights activists hoped for,
the Supreme Court decided that the case was moot and issued a per
curiam opinion, the kind of unsigned opinion of the entire Court rarely

---

[12]See Brief of Senators Sheldon Whitehouse, Maize Hirono, Richard Blumenthal, Richard
Durbin, and Kirsten Gillibrand as Amici Curiae in support of respondents (12 August 2019);
see also Sheldon Whitehouse, "The Supreme Court Has Become Just Another Arm of the
GOP," *The Washington Post* (6 September 2019).

uses in major cases. It said that the case was moot because the City had provided "the precise relief that petitioners requested in the prayer for relief in their complaint."[13]

As to the new issues raised after the litigation was filed, the Court observed that "in instances where the mootness is attributable to a change in the legal framework governing the case, and where the plaintiff may have some residual claim under the new framework that was understandably not asserted previously, our practice is to vacate the judgment and remand for further proceedings in which the parties may, if necessary, amend their pleadings or develop the record more fully."[14]

In another move likely to draw conservatives' ire, the Chief Justice sided with the Court's four liberals.[15] While Roberts had signaled his views on gun rights by joining both the *Heller* and *McDonald* majorities, during his confirmation process he allied himself with Bickel's brand of legal conservativism. There he called on Justices to pay particular attention to the Court's institutional standing and legitimacy. His tenure as Chief Justice has been marked by occasional departures from conservative orthodoxy of the kind he displayed in the New York gun case. Yet, it may not be a guide to his attitude toward future expansions of Second Amendment rights.

Justice Kavanaugh's Promise

Agreeing that the New York case was moot, Justice Kavnaugh continued his alliance with Roberts.[16] But he also used his brief concurrence to signal his allegiance to the gun rights cause.

As an appellate court judge Kavanaugh had consistently provided a pro-gun vote.[17] There he dissented in *Heller v. District of Columbia*

---

[13] *New York State Rifle & Pistol* decision Page 1.

[14] Ibid. at 2.

[15] See Josh Gerstein, "Conservatives Blast Roberts as Turncoat," *Politico* (27 June 2019).

[16] Richard Wolf, "Conservatives' Takeover of Supreme Court Stalled by John Roberts-Brett Kavanaugh Bromance," *USA Today* (7 April 2019).

[17] Mark Overstreet, "Is Kavanaugh, the Supreme Court, or the First Circuit Right About the Second Amendment?" *The Federalist* (18 November 2019).

("Heller II"), which upheld the District's "assault weapon" ban. Echoing Scalia, he asserted that "*Heller* and *McDonald* leave little doubt that courts are to assess gun bans and regulations based on text, history, and tradition, not by a balancing test such as strict or intermediate scrutiny."[18]

Kavanaugh equated the Second Amendment with the First Amendment guarantee of free speech. He called gun ownership a fundamental right that can be limited only in the narrowest of circumstances: "A ban on a class of arms is not an incidental regulation. It is equivalent to a ban on a category of speech."[19]

Thus it was not surprising that in his NYSRPA concurrence he displayed impatience with federal and state courts which failed to protect gun rights and stated his belief that "some federal and state courts may not be properly applying *Heller* and *McDonald*."[20]

Like Roberts, Kavanaugh seems to believe that the Court has little to lose and something to gain by waiting for a case that is not open to the kind of criticism launched by the senators' brief. Thus he went out of his way to note that the Court would get another chance to expand gun rights "soon, perhaps in one of the several Second Amendment cases with petitions for certiorari now pending before the Court."[21]

Alito Leads the Charge for Pro-Gun Justices

The dissenting opinion authored by Justice Alito (joined by Gorsuch and Thomas) also may give clear indication of the future of the Court's Second Amendment jurisprudence. It eschewed judicial modesty and insisted that in order for a case to be moot, it must "really be dead."[22] Because the repeal of the New York City Ordinance left some possible

---

[18]See *Heller v. District of Columbia*, US Court of Appeals for the D.C. Circuit. No. 10-7036 (2011), page 6.
[19]Ibid. at 27.
[20]Kavanaugh concurrence, page 1.
[21]Ibid.
[22]Alito dissent page 12.

restrictions in place, the Court should have reached the merits of the case. "The new City ordinance," Alito wrote,

> has limitations that petitioners claim are unconstitutional, namely, that a trip outside the City must be "direc[t]" and travel within the City must be "continuous and uninterrupted." Exactly what these restrictions mean is not clear from the face of the rule, and the City has done little to clarify their reach. At argument, counsel told us that the new rule allows "bathroom breaks," "coffee stops," and any other "reasonably necessary" stops in the course of travel." But the meaning of a "reasonably necessary" stop is hardly clear...[23]

Alito offered a hypothetical which insists that the right to bear arms is as important as First Amendment rights. "Consider," he said,

> where acceptance of the argument adopted by the *per curiam* leads. Suppose that a city council, seeking to suppress a local paper's opposition to some of its programs, adopts an ordinance prohibiting the publication of any editorial without the approval of a city official. Suppose that a newspaper challenges the constitutionality of this rule, arguing that the First Amendment confers the unrestricted right to editorialize without prior approval. If the council then repeals its ordinance and replaces it with a new one requiring approval only if the editorial concerns one particular city program, would that render the pending lawsuit moot and require the paper to commence a new one?[24]

Alito accused New York City of manufacturing mootness "in order to evade review" and warned that similar things might happen on other issues near and dear to the Court's conservative Justices. As he put it,

> One might have thought that the City, having convinced the lower courts that its law was consistent with *Heller*, would have been willing to defend its victory in this Court. But once we granted certiorari, both the City and the State of New York sprang into action to prevent us from deciding this case. Although the City had previously insisted that its ordinance

---

[23] Ibid. at 4.
[24] Ibid. at 23.

served important public safety purposes, our grant of review apparently led to an epiphany of sorts, and the City quickly changed its ordinance.[25]

To make his message abundantly clear, he speculated about what states might do to manufacture mootness in cases involving abortion and reproductive rights.

> [T]take this example. A State enacts a law providing that any woman wishing to obtain an abortion must submit certification from five doctors that the procedure is medically necessary. After a woman sues, claiming that any requirement of physician certification is unconstitutional, the State replaces its old law with a new one requiring certification by three physicians. Would the court be required to dismiss the woman's suit?[26]

Alito claimed that judges only should refuse to rule on the merits if it is "*impossible* for a court to grant *any effectual relief whatever* to the prevailing party."[27] The italics were his, calling attention to his desire to stretch the Court's jurisdiction to its limits.

Finally, Alito used his dissent to announce his views of the merits of New York City's gun regulation. He stated, "the City ordinance violated the Second Amendment. This is not a close question" and that the City's transport ban involves "core Second Amendment rights."[28] Like Scalia, Alito sees gun rights as providing a bulwark against government tyranny as well as being made necessary by government's frequent failure to protect individuals (especially women) from violence.[29] As he puts it, the New York ordinance interfered with "the right to keep a handgun in the home for self-defense."[30]

---

[25] Ibid. at 13.

[26] Ibid. at 23.

[27] Ibid. at 3.

[28] Ibid. at 25.

[29] Thanks to Morgan Marietta for pointing this out and noting that Justice Alito used a concurrence in a previous case to argue that without the right to possess a gun for self- defense "the safety of all Americans is left to the mercy of state authorities who may be more concerned about disarming the people than about keeping them safe" *Caetano v. Massachusetts*, 577 U.S. ___ (2016).

[30] Alito dissent page 10.

In his view, the City's arguments about the extent to which the transport ban protects public safety, "were weak on their face, were not substantiated in any way, and were accepted below with no serious probing." Alito believes that such laxity is typical of the way that *Heller* has been applied in the lower courts. As a result, he noted, "there is cause for concern."[31]

Conservative Judicial Activism and the Future of Gun Rights

Alito's expansive view of the Supreme Court's ability to resolve the New York gun case, as well as his contention that it made a serious mistake in not deciding on what he sees as core Second Amendment rights, signals an impending conservative judicial activism with respect to gun rights. It is reminiscent of what critics of *Heller* found wanting in that decision, namely its failure to defer to the judgments of elected officials. One critic equated *Heller* with *Roe v. Wade* and complained of "the Court's failure to adhere to a conservative judicial methodology in reaching its decision." *Heller* encouraged Americans "to do what conservative jurists warned for years they should not do: bypass the ballot and seek to press their political agenda in the courts."[32]

It is not easy to say with certainty what makes a Supreme Court decision "activist" or that an activist decision is necessarily a bad one.[33] But scholars and commentators continue to deploy that label to describe judicial decisions driven by a political agenda, judges' failure to follow the clear language of the law, their disregard of precedent and willingness to "[strike] down the actions of other parts of government... [and]

---

[31] Ibid. at 31.
[32] See J. Harvie Wilkinson, "Of Guns, Abortions, and the Unraveling Rule of Law," *Virginia Law Review* 95 (2009): 253.
[33] Elizabeth H. Slattery, "How to Spot Judicial Activism: Three Recent Examples," Legal Memorandum (Washington, DC: The Heritage Foundation, 13 June 2013).

preempt the democratic process."[34] That willingness has long been a part of Alito's approach to the Second Amendment.

While gun control advocates claimed victory in this ruling,[35] there are now a dozen gun rights cases pending before the Supreme Court, several of which challenge state laws banning assault weapons or limiting concealed carry.[36] None of them seems plagued by problems like mootness. As a result, we "soon" will see whether the Supreme Court uses one of them to decide what the Second Amendment allows in the way of limitation on gun rights.

---

[34]See for example, Cass R. Sunstein, *Radicals in Robes* (New York: Basic Books 2005), pages 42–43.

[35]See Matt Cohen, "The Supreme Court's Punt on a Second Amendment Case Is a Short-Term Victory for Gun Control Groups," *Mother Jones* (27 April 2020).

[36]See Maryland Shall Issue Lawsuit Tracker, http://www.marylandshallissue.org/jmain/counselor-s-corner/natl-litigation-trk.

12

Ramos v. Louisiana on Unanimous Juries

David Klein

Under the Constitution, must a jury's guilty verdict be unanimous? In *Ramos v. Louisiana* the Supreme Court said Yes. Because only ten of the twelve jurors in Evangelisto Ramos's trial voted to convict him of second-degree murder, his conviction was invalid, and Louisiana must either hold a new trial or let him go.

Justice Neil Gorsuch, author of the Court's principal opinion, treated the unanimity question as an easy one. This is not because the Constitution explicitly requires unanimity. The amendment in question here, the Sixth, guarantees only "an impartial jury of the State and district wherein the crime shall have been committed."[1] What Gorsuch and five

---

[1] The right to trial by jury does not extend to all criminal cases. The Court has ruled that defendants can be tried without a jury for "petty" offenses, defined as those where the maximum possible sentence is no more than six months' imprisonment (*Baldwin v. NY*, 399 U.S. 66 [1970]). The matters discussed in this chapter apply only to prosecutions for "serious" offenses, when there is a right to a jury trial.

D. Klein (✉)
Eastern Michigan University, Ypsilanti, MI, USA

© The Author(s) 2021
M. Marietta (ed.), *SCOTUS 2020*,
https://doi.org/10.1007/978-3-030-53851-4_12

other Justices found so compelling was history: for many years before and after the Sixth Amendment was ratified in 1791, pretty much everyone in America and Britain understood a jury verdict to require unanimity. Here are two examples cited by the majority in *Ramos:* in 1769, William Blackstone, an eminent authority on English law, wrote that guilt must "be confirmed by the unanimous suffrage of twelve of his equals and neighbors"; in 1898, the US Supreme Court spoke of the defendant's "constitutional right to demand that his liberty should not be taken from him except by the joint action of the court and the unanimous verdict of a jury of twelve persons."[2]

Doubtless a great many Americans will agree, not only that verdicts must be unanimous, but that this is an easy call. The unanimity requirement remains deeply ingrained in both the popular culture and legal practice of the United States. Indeed, only two states—Louisiana and Oregon—allowed nonunanimous verdicts at the time of the Court's decision.

Nevertheless, there were significant obstacles to deciding in Ramos' favor, as reflected in the fact that three Justices (Alito, Kagan, and Roberts) dissented and the six Justices in the majority produced four separate opinions. The Court in this case was not writing on a clean slate, and there were precedents favoring Louisiana. Most importantly, in *Apodaca v. Oregon* (1972), five Justices had held that state courts' jury verdicts do *not* have to be unanimous.[3] To understand why three Justices in *Ramos* voted to reaffirm *Apodaca* while six chose to reject it, we need to begin with a careful exploration of *Apodaca* itself and two cases decided shortly before it. In the course of that exploration, we will see that an apparently simple question about juries in fact implicates deep issues of *federalism* and *precedent*.

---

[2] *Thompson v. Utah*, 170 U.S. 343 at 351.
[3] 406 U.S. 404 (1972).

Williams and *Apodaca*

Two years before *Apodaca,* the Court had to decide whether juries must have twelve members. At the time, roughly a fifth of the states employed juries smaller than twelve in at least some criminal trials.[4] In *Williams v. Florida,* the majority noted that the standard jury of twelve dated all the way back to the fourteenth century but denied that this was sufficient reason to read a requirement of twelve into the Sixth Amendment. They pointed out that, while James Madison's initial draft of the Sixth Amendment specified "an impartial jury of freeholders of the vicinage, with the requisite of unanimity for conviction, of the right of challenge, and other accustomed requisites," the final version omitted the references to freeholders, unanimity, challenge, and "other accustomed requisites." They saw this as an indication that the Framers did not wish to tie future generations to a specific conception of the jury. Accordingly, a requirement of twelve jurors should only be read into the Sixth Amendment if it was an "indispensable" feature of a jury trial.

The majority in *Williams* concluded that it was not. "The purpose of the jury trial," they wrote, "is to prevent oppression by the Government." This is accomplished through "the interposition between the accused and his accuser of the common sense judgment of a group of laymen [and] the community participation and shared responsibility that results from that group's determination of guilt or innocence." In their view, the jury's ability to serve this role "is not a function of the particular number" of jurors.[5]

When the Court faced the question of unanimity in *Apodaca,* four Justices approvingly cited the analysis from *Williams* and concluded that unanimity, like the twelve-person jury, is not essential. When it comes to achieving its function, they said, "we perceive no difference between juries required to act unanimously and those permitted to convict or acquit by votes of 10 to two or 11 to one."[6]

---

[4] *Williams v. Florida,* 399 U.S. 78 (1970) fn. 45.

[5] Ibid. at 100. Several years later, the Court would establish six as the minimum size for a jury in *Ballew v. Georgia,* 435 U.S. 223 (1978).

[6] *Apodaca,* 406 U.S. 404 at 411.

Five Justices disagreed with them, holding that the Sixth Amendment imported the requirement of unanimity. But then how were there five votes to allow nonunanimous verdicts in state trials? Here we enter the land of "incorporation."

Incorporation

Although it is some of the most bewildering territory in constitutional law, incorporation grew from a straightforward proposition: the Bill of Rights was meant to restrain the newly created *national* government, not state governments. The Supreme Court so held in 1833, and it has never deviated from this holding.[7] As strange as this proposition may seem to many today, it is widely accepted by legal practitioners and scholars. When the Constitution came into effect, state governments were already powerful and already subject to constraints outlined in their own constitutions. The most important structural change accomplished by the Constitution was the replacement of the very weak central government of the Articles of Confederation with one strong enough to do good things like "provide for the common defense" and "promote the general Welfare" but also strong enough to repress people if its power was misused. The addition of the amendments that we call the Bill of Rights was a concession to those who feared the new central government would be too strong. Their target appears in the very first words of the First Amendment: "Congress shall make no law."

Today nearly every provision of the Bill of Rights is understood to constrain state governments as well. But technically their effect is not direct; rather, they operate on states by way of the Fourteenth Amendment, which was ratified shortly after the Civil War to protect people from misbehavior by state governments. It is this application of rights from the first eight amendments through the fourteenth that we call

---

[7] *Barron v. Baltimore*, 32 U.S. 243 (1833).

"incorporation." Incorporation did not begin until well into the twentieth century and proceeded in a piecemeal fashion.[8] Notably, most rights of criminal defendants were not held applicable against the states before the 1960s. For instance, the "self-incrimination" clause of the Fifth Amendment was not incorporated until 1964.[9] The Sixth Amendment's right to a criminal jury trial was first made applicable against states in 1968, and two Justices dissented from the decision.[10]

It was only four years later that the Court addressed unanimity in *Apodaca*. From our perspective nearly fifty years later, holding states to the specifics of the Bill of Rights may seem routine and obvious. But even to this day the Supreme Court has not settled on one clear approach to deciding which provisions should apply against the states and why (and to this day the Court has not incorporated the Fifth Amendment's right to indictment by a grand jury or the Seventh Amendment's right to jury trial in noncriminal cases). At the time of *Apodaca*, incorporation doctrine was in even greater flux, and the legal community was more divided. Skeptics of incorporation were especially concerned that by imposing uniformity, incorporation would deprive the country of a key benefit of federalism—the ability to try out different solutions to problems and learn from states' various experiences.

It is in this context that we can understand the decisive fifth vote in *Apodaca*. On the one hand, Justice Lewis Powell (on the Court from 1971 to 1987) agreed with four other Justices that the Sixth Amendment requires unanimity and, therefore, that verdicts in *federal* criminal trials must be unanimous. However, beginning from a position accepted by many Justices—that states are not bound by specific provisions simply because they appear in the Bill of Rights, but are bound only by those that protect fundamental rights—he asked whether unanimity is fundamental to a fair trial process. Believing that it is not, and that society benefits from allowing states to experiment with different procedures, he concluded that the Fourteenth Amendment did not require unanimity and, therefore, that verdicts in *state* trials may be divided. His vote,

---

[8] For another application of incorporation, see Chapter 12 of *SCOTUS 2019*, "*Timbs v. Indiana* on Excessive Fines and Civil Forfeitures" by Marian Williams.
[9] *Malloy v. Hogan*, 378 U.S. 1 (1964).
[10] *Duncan v. Louisiana*, 391 U.S. 145 (1968).

together with those of the four Justices who thought unanimity was not required even in federal cases, allowed Oregon and Louisiana to maintain their practice for nearly fifty more years, until the Court ended it in *Ramos*.

Ramos and *Stare Decisis*

Supreme Court Justices do not consider themselves obligated to decide questions as their predecessors did. But that does not mean that they take precedents lightly. For one thing, they recognize that careful analysis of what other smart people have said about an issue is a good way to test one's own ideas. More importantly, courts' effectiveness depends on maintaining a high degree of consistency. When courts make decisions and give reasons for them, those decisions and reasons are not meant only to resolve the immediate case; their larger function is to provide rules and principles to guide the behavior of others. When a court ignores or overrules one of its own decisions, it pulls the rug from under those who relied on the precedent to decide what they should or shouldn't do.[11] If a court does this often enough, it can undermine confidence in and respect for its rulings and even for the court itself.

These considerations have given rise to a norm called *stare decisis* (Latin for "let the decision stand" or "to stand by things decided"), which holds that mere disagreement with a precedent is not sufficient to justify overruling it. The Justices differ as to exactly which factors should be taken into account in deciding whether to overrule, and they frequently accuse each other of flouting the norm in practice, but all profess to accept it, at least in theory.

Justice Gorsuch tried to avoid the force of *stare decisis* by arguing that *Apodaca* was not actually a precedent. His argument is complicated, but it begins with the fact that no other Justice agreed with the reasons Justice Powell gave for his decisive vote in *Apodaca*. The question of what constitutes precedent when no single opinion commands a majority is a

---

[11]See the discussion of *reliance interests* in the introduction and the discussion of *precedent* in Chapter 7 on abortion regulation in *June Medical Services*.

fascinating one for aficionados of judicial decision-making, and interested readers can find an extensive debate in section IV.A of the Gorsuch opinion and section II of the dissent. For our purposes it is sufficient to note that only Justices Breyer and Ginsburg agreed with Gorsuch on this point. Since a majority felt that *Apodaca* was precedent, the crucial question was whether reasons for overruling it outweighed considerations of *stare decisis*.

The more deeply flawed a precedent is, the more justification there is for overruling it, and the Justices in *Ramos* devoted considerable space to *Apodaca's* merits. As noted in the introduction to this chapter, the Justices in the majority felt that historical practice weighed very heavily in favor of unanimity. Several of them also felt that any case for deviating from that practice was undercut by the apparently racist origins of nonunanimous verdicts in Louisiana and Oregon. Writing separately, Justices Gorsuch, Sonia Sotomayor, and Brett Kavanaugh each highlighted historical evidence that Louisiana and Oregon switched from unanimous to nonunanimous verdicts in order to maintain white domination of juries once it became difficult to keep African Americans from serving on them.

The dissenters argued that the origins of Louisiana's and Oregon's laws (in the 1890s and 1930s, respectively) are not relevant now. States' contemporary justifications are very different, focusing primarily on costs: the unanimity requirement is more likely to result in a hung jury, when the state must either retry or release the defendant. Furthermore, the Court's decision in *Ramos* rules out a shift to nonunanimous verdicts for every other state as well, regardless of how good their reasons might be.[12]

The dissenters also questioned the strength of the argument from historical practice. As they pointed out, for a long time it was also accepted practice to limit jury service to men. Today we obviously do not feel bound to respect that practice. Even more to the point, the requirement of twelve jurors seems as historically grounded as the requirement of unanimity. (Attentive readers may have noticed that the statements

---

[12]Thirteen other states and Puerto Rico submitted an amicus curiae brief asking the Court to allow nonunanimous verdicts, as did Oregon. Eight states plus the District of Columbia submitted an amicus brief on the other side.

quoted earlier from Blackstone and the Court's 1898 decision both speak of a unanimous jury of twelve people.) Yet the Supreme Court in *Williams* refused to read the requirement of twelve into the Constitution. If it is okay to dispense with some elements of a jury trial as once understood, can't the unanimity requirement be questioned too? And if it is okay to convict someone through the vote of just six (unanimous) jurors, is it obviously unacceptable to allow conviction by a vote of ten jurors against two? Tellingly, England—the country from which we imported the principle of twelve unanimous jurors—has permitted nonunanimous verdicts since 1967.[13] (It is unclear from their opinions what the Justices in the *Ramos* majority think of allowing juries to have fewer than twelve members. It could be that they would be willing to revisit *Williams*. Or it could be that they view the requirement of twelve jurors as less firmly anchored in the original understanding of the jury trial than the unanimity requirement. Perhaps we will find out in the next few years.)

As interesting as the debate over *Apodaca's* merits is, it does not appear to be the decisive battleground in *Ramos*. While the dissenters called out the majority for being excessively critical, they stopped short of claiming that *Apodaca* was decided correctly. (Notably, they did not refer to the federalism concerns that so occupied the Justices in the first jury incorporation cases.) "It might be wrong, but it's not *so* wrong" is a perfectly valid argument for observing *stare decisis*, but it's not terribly compelling. What appeared to weigh more heavily for the dissenters were the consequences of overruling.

In the dissenters' view, Oregon and Louisiana justifiably relied on *Apodaca* to continue their use of nonunanimous juries for the last 48 years. With the overruling of *Apodaca*, they now face the possibility of having to retry hundreds, perhaps even thousands, of cases. This could impose an enormous burden on their court systems.

The majority responded to this concern in two ways. First, they argued that it is overstated. In his concurrence, Justice Kavanaugh opined that only cases still making their way through the state appellate process would be eligible for retrial; defendants whose appeals had already been

---

[13]Criminal Justice Act of 1967.

closed could not raise new claims that their trials were unfair. Justice Gorsuch, joined by Justices Breyer, Ginsburg, and Sotomayor, refused to commit to this position but implied that Kavanaugh was on solid ground.

The more pointed response was that the dissent's focus on states' interests missed what mattered most. In Gorsuch's words, "the dissent would have us discard a Sixth Amendment right in perpetuity rather than ask two States to retry a slice of their prior criminal cases. Whether that slice turns out to be large or small, it cannot outweigh the interest we all share in the preservation of our constitutionally promised liberties."[14]

Privileges and Immunities

Justice Clarence Thomas stayed out of the argument about competing interests, noting that, under his "approach to *stare decisis*, there is no need to decide which reliance interests are important enough to save an incorrect precedent."[15] As this language suggests, Thomas subscribes to a less restrictive version of *stare decisis* than his colleagues do. Indeed, he has for some years been the most vocal of the Justices in calling for the overruling of precedents, even ones that are long established and have been often reaffirmed.

He did not disappoint in *Ramos*, arguing that the Court's entire body of incorporation decisions rests on a faulty base. Recall that incorporation involves applying rights from the first Eight Amendments to states by way of the Fourteenth Amendment. If you search the Fourteenth Amendment for language, you'll immediately spot a strong candidate in the Privileges or Immunities Clause, which reads, "No State shall make or enforce any law which shall abridge the privileges or immunities of citizens of the United States." This can easily be understood to mean that rights against the federal government also hold against states.

But for reasons much too complicated to get into here, when the Court began the process of incorporation in the 1920s, it chose to rely

---

[14]*Ramos* decision, page 25.
[15]Thomas concurrence, fn. 1.

instead on the Due Process Clause, which forbids states to "deprive any person of life, liberty, or property without due process of law." The Court's choice has been a source of confusion and frustration to countless students, teachers, lawyers, and judges since. ("A law that provides state funding to religious schools violates due process? What? How?") Surely many of them would agree with Justice Thomas that incorporation is more logically grounded in the Privileges and Immunities Clause than in Due Process. Still, it is also easy enough to understand why none of the other Justices were willing to join him, as there's probably not much to be gained from making a course correction this far downstream. It may also be that some have qualms about what Thomas clearly sees as a virtue of the Privileges and Immunities Clause—that it refers only to "citizens," while the Due Process Clause covers the broader category of "person[s]."[16]

Conclusion

In requiring unanimous guilty verdicts in state courts as well as federal, the Court in *Ramos* only shifted (or, depending on your perspective, returned) the law to what most Americans probably thought it already was or should be. The decision is, of course, important in practical terms, especially for defendants and some inmates in Louisiana and Oregon. In legal terms, it is less likely to be remembered for its impact on doctrine than for the insight it provides into how the Court can and should deal with problematic precedents.

---

[16]Ibid. at 8.

13

Seila Law v. Consumer Finance Protection Bureau on Separation of Powers

Howard Schweber

In 2011, in the aftermath of the catastrophic Great Recession of 2008, Congress established the Consumer Finance Protection Bureau. Like many administrative agencies, the CFPB was designed to be independent, with a head who served a five-year term and could only be removed for "inefficiency, neglect of duty, or malfeasance in office," rather than serving at the pleasure of the President. In the first decade of its operation, the CFPB brought numerous actions against financial institutions, recovering more than $11 billion in damages for the US Treasury. In 2017 the CFPB brought an action against the Seila Law Firm looking for some documents relating to a series of financial transactions. Seila Law Firm sued, arguing that the structure of the agency was unconstitutional. The case went all the way to the Supreme Court, which ultimately agreed: The creation of an agency with a single head who could not be removed at will by the President violated the Constitution.

This might seem like a remarkably arid controversy around a technical question. In fact, *Seila Law* considers some of the oldest constitutional

H. Schweber (✉)
University of Wisconsin-Madison, Madison, WI, USA

© The Author(s) 2021
M. Marietta (ed.), *SCOTUS 2020*,
https://doi.org/10.1007/978-3-030-53851-4_13

questions in the American canon. What is at stake is a basic question about separation of powers, checks and balances, and the nature of the Executive Branch. To see why requires looking briefly at the historical background to the issues involved.

The History of Removal Power Controversies

Article II provides that the "executive Power shall be vested in a President." But because it would be "impossib[le]" for "one man" to "perform all the great business of the State," the Constitution assumes that lesser executive officers will "assist the supreme Magistrate in discharging the duties of his trust."[1] The question is who controls the process of appointing and removing these executive officers?

The Constitution provides for the appointment of executive branch officials in the Appointments Clause: Art. II, sec. 2, which provides that the President shall nominate "officers of the United States," who shall be appointed subject to the advice and consent of the Senate. In addition, "Congress may by law vest the appointment of such inferior officers, as they think proper, in the President alone, in the courts of law, or in the heads of departments." There is a noticeable hole in the clause. It describes the process of appointment, but not of removal. Scholars who have reviewed the record closely conclude that "the Framers" thought that these and many other questions would be worked out in the future. It did not take long for the question of removal authority under the Appointments Clause to emerge: in 1789 the First Congress was fixated on the issue.

In James Madison's view, the power to remove officials was an essential mechanism to protect the Executive branch from being taken over by Congress. Madison argued that requiring a President to accept subordinate executive officials who displayed a "lack of loyalty" would "thwart

---

[1] *Writings of George Washington* (ed. J. Fitzpatrick), vol. 30, page 334 (1939).

the Executive in the exercise... of his great responsibility."[2] In addition, Madison argued that giving the President control over all executive officers would enhance accountability, as the President could be held accountable by the voters for the actions of his government.

Others disagreed. Some argued that since the constitutional text did not provide a mechanism for removal, executive positions carried life tenure subject to impeachment. For James Jackson of Georgia, this was critical in preventing the President from usurping Congress' power of the purse. "If he [the president] has the power of removing and controlling the treasury department, he has the purse strings in his hand."[3] Elbridge Gerry took the position that the process of removal should be the same as the process of appointment, relying on the advice and consent of the Senate except in the case of "inferior officers."[4] And yet a fourth theory held that the silence of the text implied Congress had authority to delegate to the President the power of removal or to refrain from doing so in all cases.

The problem that faced the First Congress was a conceptual one that frequently creates confusion in modern discussions. There is a common tendency even among Supreme Court Justices to talk about separation of powers and checks and balances as though they are equivalent concepts. In fact, they are very nearly opposite. "Separation of powers" is the idea that each branch should be supreme within its ambit, without being subject to interference from the other two. "Checks and balances" are created when powers *overlap*: Congress has the power to make laws, but the President has the power of veto, but Congress has the power of override; Congress has power over expenditures, but the Executive has discretion over the process of spending the money; Congress can create criminal and administrative laws, but the Executive has discretion over

---

[2]"The chain of dependence therefore terminates in the supreme body, namely, in the people." James Madison, "Speech in Congress on Presidential Removal Power," in Madison, *Writings* (Library of America 1999), 456.

[3]Linda De Pauw et al., *Documentary History of the First Federal Congress of the United States of America, March 4, 1789–March 3, 1791 "DHFFC"* (Johns Hopkins University Press, 1972), pages 726, 1002.

[4]Ibid. at 1022–1023.

their enforcement. And in all of this the courts act as referees in the never-ending struggle between the legislative and executive branches.

The "Decision of 1789," as it is known, was inconclusive. Proposed Executive departments were approved, but the general question was left unresolved.[5] As a result the question arose again during the Jackson administration. At odds with Congress over the propriety of a national Bank, Jackson ordered his Secretary of the Treasury to remove all federal deposits. In a moment with foreshadowings of Watergate's "Saturday Night Massacre" the Secretary of the Treasury, William J. Duane, refused to carry out the order, so Jackson fired him and replaced him with Attorney General Roger Taney, who was rewarded for his loyalty with an appointment as Chief Justice of the Supreme Court in 1835.[6] Jackson's opponents in Congress argued that he had no authority to give the order to remove deposits in the first place. They pointed out that the Bank charter gave the Secretary of the Treasury, not the President, the authority to make federal deposits; they argued and implied that only the Secretary of the Treasury could remove such deposits. In response, Jackson articulated the theory of the "unitary executive"; since the President controlled the appointment and removal of executive officers, all their actions were his actions and subject to his control.[7]

The political environment of removal controversies changed as the federal government expanded dramatically beginning in the late 1870s.[8] One of the driving forces behind the growth of executive agencies was the Progressives' belief in the efficacy of regulatory executive agencies.[9] The Progressive ideal involved disinterested experts providing sound policy mandates based on nonpolitical considerations. As a result, it was

---

[5]J. David Alvis et al., *The Contested Removal Power, 1789–2010* (Lawrence KS: University Press of Kansas, 2013).

[6]Taney went on to write the infamous ruling in *Dred Scott* in 1857 that Blacks were not citizens of the United States and "had no rights which the white man was bound to respect," rejecting the Missouri Compromise preceding the Civil War.

[7]Mark Graber, Howard Gillman, and Keith Whittington, *American Constitutionalism* vol. 1 (2 vols.) (Oxford University Press), page 230.

[8]Stephen Skowronek, *Building a New American State: the Expansion of National Administrative Capacities 1877–1920* (New York: Cambridge University Press, 1981); Michael Nelson, "A Short, Ironic History of American National Bureaucracy," *The Journal of Politics* 44 (1982): 747–778.

[9]Thomas M. McCraw, *Prophets of Regulation* (Belknap Press, 1986).

essential that these agencies be independent of both the President and the Congress. Numerous modern agencies display this independence; perhaps the most notable example is the Federal Reserve.

Removal Power in the Supreme Court

Two major cases in the twentieth century defined the competing constitutional positions. In *Myers* v. *United States* the Court was asked whether President Wilson could unilaterally dismiss the Postmaster of Portland, Oregon.[10] Chief Justice Taft ruled that the power of dismissal was implied by the Constitution's vesting of "executive" powers in the President, and (echoing Jackson) that Executive branch officials—including all agency heads or commissioners—were essentially the President's staff and served to carry out his bidding.

Commentators immediately pointed out that *Myers* threatened the entire national system of government.[11] Sure enough, nine years later in *Humphrey's Executor* v. *United States* in 1935 the Court revisited the question.[12] The Federal Trade Act of 1914 provided that members of the Federal Trade Commission could be removed by a President only for "inefficiency, neglect of duty, or malfeasance in office." In upholding the law, the Court introduced a new, function-based distinction between purely executive agencies and those that were "quasi-legislative" or "quasi-judicial." The Court found that the FTC was not a purely executive agency because it carried out policymaking and the adjudication of claims, and therefore its members could be shielded from removal without cause. Justice Sutherland's opinion for a unanimous Court was a perfect expression of the Progressive ideal: "The commission is to be nonpartisan, and it must, from the very nature of its duties, act with entire impartiality. It is charged with the enforcement of no policy except the policy of the law...its members are called upon to exercise the

---

[10]272 U.S. 52 (1926).
[11]Edward S. Corwin, "Tenure of Office and Removal Power Under the Constitution," *Columbia Law Review* 27 (1927): 353–397.
[12]295 U.S. 602 (1935).

trained judgment of a body of experts appointed by law and informed by experience."[13]

Later cases applied the principles of *Humphrey's Executor* to various specific situations, but the tension between the principles expressed in *Myers* and *Humphrey's Executor* provided the background for the analysis in *Seila Law*.

Seila Law v. Consumer Finance Protection Bureau

Chief Justice Roberts authored a majority opinion that alluded to nearly all the arguments that have been mentioned so far, and a few more besides. Roberts embraced a version of the unitary executive theory: "Under our Constitution, the 'executive Power'—all of it—is vested in a President…Without such power, the President could not be held fully accountable for discharging his own responsibilities; the buck would stop somewhere else." By contrast, an independent agency with a single head meant no effective accountability at all. "The Director is neither elected by the people nor meaningfully controlled (through the threat of removal) by someone who is."[14]

The single director structure was key. Roberts claimed this design was inconsistent with the theory of regulatory entities which were designed to ensure "non-partisan[ship]" and "impartiality," eliciting the "trained judgment of a body of experts." Progressives had promoted commissions on the grounds that they would remain independent of both the President and Congress; for Roberts, the structure of the CFPB meant that its leadership might be *too* independent of the President. "A President elected in 2020 would likely not appoint a CFPB Director until 2023, and a President elected in 2028 may *never* appoint one. That means an unlucky President might get elected on a consumer-protection platform

---

[13] *Humphrey's Executor*, 295 U.S. at 624.
[14] *Seila Law* decision, page 23.

and enter office only to find herself saddled with a holdover Director from a competing political party ....”[15]

Unlike the FTC commissioners in *Humphrey's Executor*, Roberts found, the Director of the CFPB performed executive functions in that he had authority to promulgate binding rules and issue rulings awarding "legal and equitable relief." Roberts did not explain how these roles constitute traditional executive functions, but said that the result was to deprive the President of authority to determine how laws should be executed and thus interfered with the performance of his constitutional duties. As a result, unlike the several commission members in *Humphrey's Executor*, a single head of the CFPB must be subject to removal by a President "based on disagreements about agency policy" rather than only on a showing of poor performance of her duties.[16] Roberts insisted that past cases that permitted the creation of independent agencies were the exception that proved the rule of removal at will. As a result, the structure of the CFPB was unconstitutional; Congress could retain the Board by moving to a commission model, or by granting the President the authority to remove the director at will.

Justice Thomas wrote an opinion calling for *Humphrey's Executor* to be overruled, and for all independent and inter-branch agencies to be abolished in order to restore a pure system of separation of powers. "The Constitution sets out three branches of Government and provides each with a different form of power—legislative, executive, and judicial. Free-floating agencies simply do not comport with this constitutional structure."[17]

Justice Kagan wrote an opinion that can best be described as an evisceration of Roberts' arguments. The majority's account, she wrote, "is wrong in every respect. The majority's general rule does not exist. Its exceptions, likewise, are made up for the occasion—gerrymandered so the CFPB falls outside them. And the distinction doing most of the

---

[15]Ibid. at 14–15, 24.
[16]Ibid. at 16–17, 28.
[17]Thomas concurrence, page 10.

majority's work—between multimember bodies and single directors—does not respond to the constitutional values at stake."[18]

To begin with, Kagan went straight for the core question of constitutional theory, accusing Roberts of employing a simplistic "Schoolhouse Rock" version of separation of powers. As Kagan pointed out, separation of powers has to be balanced against the need for checks and balances: "James Madison stated the creation of distinct branches 'did not mean that these departments ought to have no partial agency in, or no control over the acts of each other.' To the contrary, Madison explained, the drafters of the Constitution—like those of then-existing state constitutions—opted against keeping the branches of government 'absolutely separate and distinct' (quoting *Federalist* 47.) Or as Justice Story reiterated a half-century later: '[W]hen we speak of a separation of the three great departments of government,' it is 'not meant to affirm, that they must be kept wholly and entirely separate.' Instead, the branches have—as they must for the whole arrangement to work—'common link[s] of connexion [and] dependence.'"[19]

Kagan rejected Roberts' idea that independent agencies represent an exception to a larger rule. Kagan cited a long history, going back to the founding, of Congress creating agencies whose heads were immune from removal by the President without cause under the authority of the Necessary and Proper Clause of Article I, Sect. 8. "The text of the Constitution, the history of the country, the precedents of this Court, and the need for sound and adaptable governance—all stand against the majority's opinion. They point not to the majority's 'general rule' of 'unrestricted removal power' with two grudgingly applied 'exceptions.' Rather, they bestow discretion on the legislature to structure administrative institutions as the times demand, so long as the President retains the ability to carry out his constitutional duties."[20]

As for Roberts' emphasis on the existence of a single agency head rather than a commission, Kagan referred to this as a form of intellectual "gerrymandering" designed to find a way to take the case out

---

[18] Kagan dissent, page 3.
[19] Ibid. at 5.
[20] Ibid. at 4.

of the reach of the mainstream principle. "The majority picks out that until-now-irrelevant fact to distinguish the CFPB, and constructs around it an until-now-unheard-of exception."[21] Moreover, as Kagan pointed out, the logic of the majority's argument—that a single-headed agency would be too independent of the President—contradicted the realities of administrative operations. Kagan proposed that a single agency head was more subject to presidential control than an equally nonremovable panel of commissioners. Furthermore, Kagan argued, a President retains numerous ways of influencing an agency short of the threat of removal. To Kagan, this illustrated the reason courts should stay out of applying rules to limit the ability of Congress to create different kinds of agencies. "Compared to Congress and the President, the Judiciary possesses an inferior understanding of the realities of administration" and the way "political power operates."[22]

The Removal Power and the Future of Separation of Powers

The specific ruling in *Seila Law* is narrow; one particular model of agency organization is prohibited. The larger principle, however, points to the ongoing conflict between Congress and the President over control of federal policy. In this area as in others, President Trump has pushed the envelope of accepted past practice in ways that bring the issues into sharp relief, relying on "acting" appointments to avoid advice and consent requirements, asserting a particularly strict version of the unitary executive, and at least appearing to try to convert traditionally independent agencies—particularly those involved in matters of public health and medical science—to instruments of his political will. Whatever one's take on President Trump's actions, the issues raised in *Seila Law* are obviously very far from resolved.

One way to think about those issues might be in terms of a commonly used phrase, "elections have consequences." The statement is a truism,

---

[21] Ibid. at 30, 32.
[22] Ibid. at 1.

but it also raises a profound question about American democracy in the modern era. While Congress remains the legislative branch, the vast majority of national governance is carried out by executive agencies. To what extent is it constitutionally required or desirable that the entire approach of the national government should be subject to abrupt and wrenching change every four years? Conversely, to what extent is it constitutionally permitted or desirable that the "effects" of an election—an expression of a desire for a change in the policy and politics of the national government—be restrained by the appointees of a prior President? This is the problem of striking a balance between separation of powers and checks and balances as governing principles. *Seila Law* does not resolve any of these questions, but it presents them in sharp relief and reminds us that we are dealing with questions that have been central to the design of American government since the Founding.

14

Trump v. Mazars and *Trump v. Vance* on Presidential Subpoenas

Cornell Clayton and Joseph Bolton

In the midst of the 2020 presidential election, the Supreme Court handed down two politically fraught cases. *Trump v. Mazars* and *Trump v. Vance* both asked the Court to block subpoenas for President Trump's personal financial records, including tax returns he refused to disclose during the 2016 campaign.

The Court rejected President Trump's claims of executive immunity from subpoena in these cases. In remanding them for further review, however, it made it unlikely Trump's financial records would see the light of day before the presidential election.

Although both cases involved subpoenas for Trump's financial documents, they raised distinct constitutional concerns. *Mazars* is the first time the Court has addressed a congressional subpoena seeking the President's personal, nonofficial records. It raised important questions about the separation of powers and Congress' authority to investigate a sitting President. *Vance* marks the first time a state criminal grand jury issued a

C. Clayton (✉) · J. Bolton
Washington State University, Pullman, WA, USA

© The Author(s) 2021
M. Marietta (ed.), *SCOTUS 2020*,
https://doi.org/10.1007/978-3-030-53851-4_14

subpoena for records from a sitting President. It raised questions about federalism and presidential immunity from criminal investigations.

To decide these cases, the Court reexamined two landmark decisions, *U.S. v. Nixon* and *Clinton v. Jones*, which declared the President is not above the law.[1] The decisions this year reaffirmed that core principle.

The Political Context

These cases arose in a hyper-charged political environment. Trump was the first contemporary President to refuse to release his tax returns, and he faced a barrage of investigations during his first term. Only months into his presidency, Robert Mueller III was appointed as a special counsel to investigate whether Trump's presidential campaign conspired with Russians to influence the 2016 election. The two-year investigation led to prosecution of several campaign officials, though no charges against the President himself.[2]

No sooner did the Mueller investigation end, than the President was targeted in a congressional impeachment inquiry into whether he withheld military assistance from Ukraine in order to extract dirt on a political rival, Joe Biden. In December 2019, the Democratic-controlled House of Representative impeached the President, but two months later the Republican-controlled Senate acquitted him of the charges.[3]

Trump was the subject of numerous other inquiries as well, including investigations into possible violations of the Emoluments Clause, congressional investigations into obstruction of the Mueller inquiry, and a separate investigation and subpoena for Trump's tax records from the House Ways and Means Committee, which was put on hold pending the outcome of these cases.[4]

---

[1]418 U.S. 683 (1974); 520 U.S. 681 (1997).

[2]United States Department of Justice, *Report on the Investigation into Russian Interference in the 2016 Presidential Election* (2019) www.justice.gov/storage/report_volume1.pdf.

[3]United States House of Representatives, *Impeachment of Donald J. Trump, President of the United States: Report by the Committee on the Judiciary* (2019).

[4]See *Committee on the Judiciary v. McGahn*, USCA, Case No. 1:19-cv-2379; *In Re Donald Trump*, USCA4 Appeal, No. 18-2486; *Committee on the Judiciary, United States House of Representatives v. United States Department of Justice*, USCA Case #19-5288 (2020).

Throughout these investigations the Trump White House asserted expansive claims to executive privilege and presidential immunity. It refused to cooperate with investigators and rebuffed subpoenas issued to numerous administration officials. The President repeatedly denounced the investigations as partisan "witch hunts." Opponents charged he was "stonewalling."

Background of the Cases

The *Vance* case began in 2018, when the Manhattan District Attorney, Cyrus Vance, Jr., opened a criminal investigation into possible tax and financial fraud by Trump's businesses, as well as into hush-money payments made during the 2016 campaign to women alleging affairs with Trump. The grand jury served a subpoena on Mazars USA, LLP, the President's personal accounting firm, seeking his financial records from 2011 to the present, including his tax returns.

The President sued to block the subpoena, arguing that under Article II and the Supremacy Clause, a sitting President enjoys absolute immunity from state criminal process while in office. Immunity, Trump said, was required to shield Presidents from frivolous investigations and prevent their distraction from constitutional responsibilities.

A federal district court held against the President, and the US Court of Appeals for the Second Circuit relied on *United States v. Nixon* and *Clinton v. Jones* to reject Trump's petition to reverse. In *Clinton*, the Supreme Court permitted a sexual harassment civil lawsuit to proceed against the sitting President.[5] The Justices held that trial courts could protect the Executive against frivolous lawsuits and could accommodate legitimate concerns about the President's schedule. In *Nixon*, the Court upheld a subpoena in a criminal investigation seeking tape recordings

---

[5] Paula Jones accused Bill Clinton in 1994 of sexually harassing her while he was Governor of Arkansas. The proceedings led to the revelation of Clinton's affair with Monica Lewinsky and the subsequent impeachment by the House of Representatives. Clinton was acquitted by the Senate. He agreed to an out-of-court settlement in 1998 of $850,000 but maintains his innocence.

of Oval Office conversations, as well as other documents which President Nixon held in his official capacity. The Second Circuit reasoned the subpoena in *Vance* should be enforced because it required no direct action by the President nor privileged materials related to his official duties.

In appealing to the Supreme Court, Trump's lawyers argued that criminal investigations would be more distracting and stigmatizing to a President than the civil litigation in *Clinton*. They also pointed out that the subpoena in *Nixon* dealt with the prosecution of third parties (i.e., the Watergate burglars) and not an investigation of the President himself. The subpoena also came from federal prosecutors in the US Department of Justice, accountable to the President. Permitting thousands of state and local prosecutors, with no equivalent accountability, to launch criminal investigations could easily incapacitate the presidency and jeopardize federal supremacy.

In its brief supporting Trump, the Solicitor General declined to endorse categorical immunity, but said presidential subpoenas should nevertheless meet a "heightened standard of need," which had not been met in this case. That standard, used in *Nixon* and other cases involving executive privilege, requires prosecutors to demonstrate that the evidence is necessary to their investigation and cannot wait until the President leaves office.

In response, Vance argued that applying either absolute immunity or a heightened standard would effectively place the President above the law. Evidence would grow stale if investigations were delayed, and statutes of limitation would prevent relevant parties from being prosecuted for their crimes

The question presented to the Court in *Vance* was what, if any, immunity the President has from state criminal subpoenas?

The subpoena in *Mazars* was issued by the House Oversight Committee, which also sought from the President's accounting firm personal financial information dating back to 2011. At the Supreme Court, it was consolidated with a second case, *Trump v. Deutsche Bank AG*, in which the House Financial Service and House Intelligence

Committees had subpoenaed Deutsche Bank and Capital One for other financial information involving Trump businesses.[6] Congress said the information was necessary to consider legislation involving ethics laws, election integrity, national security, and abuse of the financial system. Trump argued that the investigations lacked a legitimate legislative purpose, and that he should be shielded from congressional harassment under separation of powers doctrines.

In refusing to block the subpoenas, the US Courts of Appeals for the Second and D.C. Circuits cited nearly a century of case law supporting Congress' broad power to subpoena. The Supreme Court recognized this authority as early as 1927, in *McGrain* v. *Daugherty*, where it held that the power to "investigate and… secure needed information" was inherent in the power to legislate.[7] In *Eastland v. United States Servicemen's Fund* the Court said congressional subpoenas were valid as long as they sought "information about a subject on which legislation may be had," a test highly deferential to Congress.[8] And in *Barenblatt v. United States*, the Court said that when Congress acted within its constitutional power, courts lacked standing to consider investigative motives.[9]

Mazars, however, is the first time the Court addressed a congressional subpoena for the President's personal, nonofficial records. Trump again urged a territorial view of presidential immunity, arguing that, short of impeachment, Congress has little authority to seek personal information from a sitting President. Moreover, he alleged that Congress' true purpose was not legislative but prosecutorial (to investigate whether he violated any laws), a power exclusively delegated to the executive branch. At the very least, Trump argued, the Executive must be protected from politically motivated investigations by requiring that Congress meet a higher standard of "specific need" for the information.

The Solicitor General, siding with the President, argued that even if congressional subpoenas reflected a legitimate legislative purpose, a "clear, specific statement" of that purpose was required. Otherwise, there

---

[6] *Trump v. Deutsche Bank AG*, No. 19-760.
[7] 273 U.S. 135 (1927) at 161.
[8] 421 U.S. 491 (1975).
[9] 360 U.S. 109 (1959).

were no real limits to Congress' authority. Permitting Congress to investigate every detail of a President's personal life, without a specific need, would undermine the President's independence under the Constitution.

In response, Congress argued that its power to legislate is broad, and the power to investigate equally broad, with few limitations. Trump's records were needed to consider changing federal ethics laws, and requiring Congress to articulate more specific purposes was impractical, since investigation is usually necessary before knowing what legislation should be passed. In addition, the Court should reject any Article II privilege claims because the information sought was unconnected to the President's official duties, and the President made no such claim in this case.

Mazars thus asked the Court to consider the limits of congressional investigative power, and what, if any, protection the separation of powers offers a sitting President.

The *Vance* Decision

In a 7-2 decision, the Court affirmed the decision of the Second Circuit, and held that neither Article II nor the Supremacy Clause bar a state criminal subpoena for the personal records of the President, nor do they require a heightened standard.

Writing for the Court, Chief Justice Roberts' opinion was joined by the four liberal Justices, Ginsburg, Breyer, Sotomayor, and Kagan. President Trump's two appointees to the Court, Gorsuch and Kavanaugh, concurred in the judgment. Thomas and Alito wrote dissents.

The Chief Justice wrote that "the public has a right to every man's evidence. Since the earliest days of the Republic, 'every man' has included the President of the United States."[10]

Offering a detailed account of *United States v. Burr*, Roberts wrote that as early as 1807, the great Chief Justice, John Marshall, presiding over the treason trial of Aaron Burr, rejected claims to presidential immunity

---

[10] *Vance* decision, page 1.

and upheld a subpoena to President Jefferson.[11] Presidents do not "stand exempt" from the Sixth Amendment's guarantee to obtain evidence in criminal trials, Marshall held.

In the two centuries since, presidents from Monroe to Clinton accepted Marshall's ruling and provided evidence in criminal proceedings. Bookending that history, Roberts wrote, the Court in *United States v. Nixon* held that the interests of the President must be balanced against the "countervailing public interest in fair and accurate judicial proceedings," which is at its height in the criminal setting.[12]

The Court dispensed with each of Trump's arguments for immunity. First, the idea that presidents may become distracted was explicitly rejected as a basis for immunity in *Clinton v. Jones.* Experience confirmed that properly tailored subpoenas would not interfere with the President's official duties. Second, even if a tarnished reputation were a cognizable impairment, the Court found "nothing inherently stigmatizing about the President performing 'the citizen's normal duty'" of furnishing evidence in a criminal investigation. Finally, the possibility that a President would be harassed by frivolous subpoenas also had been rejected in *Clinton.* Trial courts have plenty of tools, the Court said, "to deter and, where necessary, dismiss" vexatious suits.[13]

The Court's majority also refused to apply the "heightened need" standard from cases involving executive privilege. Such an exacting standard would be inappropriate in cases involving unprivileged materials, where the President stands in "the same situation with any other individual." Nor was there any evidence that a heightened standard was necessary to protect the presidency. Absent that need, the "public interest in fair and effective law enforcement cuts in favor of comprehensive access to evidence."[14]

Still, the President was not without protections. Like other litigants, he could challenge a subpoena on the grounds of bad faith, undue burden,

---

[11]25 F. Cas. 30, 33–34 (No. 14,692d) (CC Va. 1807).
[12]*Vance* decision, pages 8–9.
[13]Ibid. at 14, 16.
[14]Ibid. at 18, 19.

or over-breadth. Presidents could also raise subpoena-specific constitutional challenges, by showing that compliance with a particular subpoena would impede constitutional duties or violate federal supremacy.[15]

"Two hundred years ago," Roberts' concluded, "a great jurist of our Court established that no citizen, not even the President, is categorically above the common duty to produce evidence when called upon in a criminal proceeding. We reaffirm that principle today…"[16]

Justice Kavanaugh, joined by Gorsuch, concurred in the Court's judgment, though they would have applied the "demonstrated need" test from *Nixon*. They noted, however, that the Court "unanimously concludes that a President does not possess absolute immunity from a state criminal subpoena," and the Court also "unanimously agrees that this case should be remanded" so the lower court could consider specific legal objections the President might raise to the subpoena.[17]

In separate dissents, Justices Thomas and Alito also rejected the President's claim of absolute immunity, but said they would have vacated the lower court decision. Thomas expressed concern that criminal investigations would place undue demands on the President's time and a "mental burden" even when he was not personally required to provide the information.[18]

Alito feared that potential investigations by thousands of local prosecutors could threaten the function of the presidency and jeopardize federal supremacy. The dissenters would have remanded the case with instructions for the lower court to consider whether, short of categorical immunity, the "Constitution demands" a higher degree of protection for the presidency.[19]

---

[15]Quoting Joseph Story's *Commentaries on the Constitution* from 1833 and the *Clinton v. Jones* case from 1997, Roberts writes that "Incidental to the functions confided in Article II is 'the power to perform them, without obstruction or impediment.'" Hence, once a President "shows that an order or subpoena would 'significantly interfere with his efforts to carry out' those duties, 'the matter changes.' At that point, a court should use its inherent authority to quash or modify the subpoena." Ibid. at 21.

[16]Ibid.

[17]*Vance* Kavanagh concurrence, page 1.

[18]*Vance* Thomas dissent, page 12.

[19]*Vance* Alito dissent, page 24.

The *Mazars* Decision

Chief Justice Roberts also wrote the opinion for a 7-2 Court in *Mazars*, with Thomas and Alito again in dissent. The Court reaffirmed Congress' authority to subpoena information as part of its legislative function, but the Justices were unanimous in saying that power was not unlimited, and Congress needed greater justification to subpoena a President. Having failed to adequately account for the separation of powers concerns raised by such subpoenas, the decisions of the lower courts were vacated by the Court, and the cases were remanded with new criteria designed to balance those concerns.

While Congress' investigative power is indispensable, Roberts said, it is not without limits. It cannot, for example, be used for law enforcement (a power exclusive to the executive and judicial branches), or to obtain information protected by attorney client privilege or executive privilege. This case was the first time Congress subpoenaed personal, non-privileged material from the President.

The "demonstrated, specific need" standard, urged by the President and Solicitor General, came from executive privilege cases, where confidentiality of official communications was held essential to the functioning of the executive branch. But such concerns were not present in this case, Roberts wrote. Applying such an exacting standard to subpoenas for non-privileged material would unduly hamstring Congress' ability to monitor the affairs of government and inform the public about how they are being served.

At the other extreme, the House and lower courts viewed the presence of the President in this case as irrelevant. The Court could not, however, turn a blind eye to the fact that "the subpoenas do not represent a run-of-the-mill legislative effort but rather a clash between rival branches of government over records of intense political interest for all involved."[20] The deferential standards used in ordinary congressional subpoena cases (i.e., "a valid legislative purpose" from *Barenblatt*, or "a subject on which legislation could be had" from *Eastland*) underestimated the separation of powers issues when a subpoena involves the President. Without

---

[20] *Mazars* decision, pages 16–17.

limits on its power, Roberts wrote, Congress could harass the President and undo the long history of compromise and bargaining between the branches.

Vacating the lower court decisions, the Court remanded the cases with instructions that they apply a more "balanced approach."[21] At a minimum, that approach must consider several factors in evaluating Congressional subpoenas for the President's personal information, including whether the asserted legislative purpose could be met by other sources of information; whether the subpoena is tailored and "no broader than reasonably necessary"; whether the asserted legislative purpose is "detailed and substantial"; and whether compliance with the subpoena would place burdens on the President's Article II duties.

In separate dissents, Justices Thomas and Alito would have gone further. Justice Alito argued that legislative subpoenas for a President's personal documents are "inherently suspicious" and must be subject to a more careful review than the majority opinion called for, though he declined to articulate a specific standard.

Thomas argued that Congress has no general authority to subpoena the President's personal documents, which could be obtained only through the impeachment power (expressly disavowed by the House in this case). Moreover, he would have held that legislative subpoenas for private, nonofficial documents generally are beyond the scope of Congress' implied power and raise Fourth Amendment issues. He would have overturned *McGrain* and sharply curtailed Congress' subpoena power.

---

[21] "Congressional subpoenas for the President's personal information implicate weighty concerns regarding the separation of powers. Neither side, however, identifies an approach that accounts for these concerns... A balanced approach is necessary..." Ibid. at 18.

Future Implications

The Court's decisions will profoundly affect the investigations into President Trump, as well as the parameters of immunity for future presidents. As a practical matter, they allowed the legal disputes over Trump's financial records to continue, but made it unlikely his tax records would become public before the 2020 election.

Vance is the more critical loss for the presidency and Trump. The Court unanimously rejected claims to categorical immunity and refused to apply a heightened standard to subpoenas for non-privileged material. Presidents are required to provide evidence in criminal proceedings, just as other citizens. Any documents turned over in *Vance* will be covered by rules of grand jury secrecy and not be public, but the decision permits a criminal investigation into Trumps business practices to continue, which could have devastating consequences.

The *Mazars* decision also rejected the President's assertion of broad immunity, though it also unanimously rejected the House's claim of near unbounded authority to subpoena the President. The test articulated by the Chief Justice places new constraints on legislative subpoenas to the President, premised on the legislature's stated need for the documents in question. This will force Congress to be more circumspect when it issues subpoenas for the President's personal information, but it does not prevent it, and Congress will undoubtedly try again to subpoena the information it is after.

In repudiating the extreme positions of both sides in *Mazars*, the Court reasserted traditional principles of the separation of powers. The Constitution requires cooperation and the balancing of the interests of both branches, allowing neither the Congress nor the presidency to overreach the powers and prerogatives of the other.

In reaching 7-to-2 judgments in these cases, the Court also avoided the partisan divisions that afflict American society and other institutions. The Justices came to balanced decisions on questions of political significance, reaffirming the principle that no person, not even the President, is above the law.

15

Ideology and the Court's Work

Lawrence Baum

From 1993 to 2020 the Supreme Court has had five Justices who were generally perceived as conservative and four perceived as liberal.[1] Since 2010 the Court's ideological lines have coincided with party lines: all the liberal Justices were appointed to the Court by Democratic presidents, all the conservatives by Republicans. The Court's ideological split explains a great deal of what it did in the 2019 term, but ideology alone could not have predicted many of the surprising outcomes.

The standard labeling of Justices as liberal and conservative has considerable validity, but it also oversimplifies the Justices. For one thing, in many of the cases that the Court decides, the alternatives from which the Justices choose are not clearly liberal on one side and conservative

---

[1]The exception is the fourteen months between the death of Justice Antonin Scalia in February 2016 and the confirmation of his successor Neil Gorsuch in April 2017; during that time the Court was tied 4-4.

L. Baum (✉)
Ohio State University, Columbus, OH, USA

© The Author(s) 2021
M. Marietta (ed.), *SCOTUS 2020*,
https://doi.org/10.1007/978-3-030-53851-4_15

on the other. On the cases that do have liberal and conservative alternatives, every Justice casts many votes for conservative positions and many others for liberal positions. Further, Justices on one side of the ideological spectrum are not alike in their ideological positions. Chief Justice John Roberts does not have the same views as Justice Clarence Thomas, though both are surely conservatives, nor do Justice Elena Kagan and Ruth Bader Ginsburg hold the same views even as they both stand on the liberal side of the Court. Those differences can have a powerful impact on the Court's decisions.

Background of the 2019 Term

Anthony Kennedy, appointed to the Court by President Reagan, was somewhat to the left of the Court's other Republican appointees during his last eight terms on the Court. His retirement in 2018 and the appointment of Brett Kavanaugh as his successor were expected to sharpen the Court's ideological divisions. In one sense, those expectations were fulfilled in Kavanaugh's first term: the gap between the four liberals and the five conservatives in their proportions of liberal and conservative votes was considerably greater than it typically had been since 2010 (though not in Kennedy's last term on the Court).[2]

The Justices' records of votes on case outcomes—who wins and loses—provide only a partial picture of their ideological positions, because it is ultimately the legal rules they support in opinions that have the greatest impact. Still, their votes provide a systematic picture of their general positions. In cases that had clear ideological content in the preceding 2018 term, all the conservative Justices cast liberal votes less than forty percent of the time.[3] In contrast, all the liberals

[2]This comparison is based on analysis of data in the Supreme Court Database, http://scdb.wus tl.edu.

[3]On ideological voting patterns in the 2018 term, see Chapter 14 of *SCOTUS 2019*, "Justice Brett Kavanaugh Joins the Court," by Lawrence Baum. As described in that chapter (p. 149 n. 7), "in general, votes for litigants who claim that their civil liberties have been violated are characterized as liberal; votes for businesses in conflicts with consumers, employees, and government regulation are characterized as conservative." For that chapter and this one, Justices' votes were counted only in cases in which the litigants' competing positions clearly could be

cast liberal votes more than sixty-five percent of the time. But there were only seven decisions in which all the conservatives were on one side and all the liberals on the other side. Three of the conservatives— Chief Justice John Roberts, Justice Neil Gorsuch, and Kavanaugh—each joined the liberal Justices in three or four cases to create 5-4 or 6-3 votes for liberal outcomes. As that figure suggests, among the Court's Republican appointees Clarence Thomas and Samuel Alito were distinctly more conservative in the 2018 term than Roberts, Gorsuch, and Kavanaugh. Among the Democratic appointees, Sonia Sotomayor and Ruth Bader Ginsburg were distinctly more liberal than Stephen Breyer and Elena Kagan.

The 2018 term was transitional. The Court heard relatively few high-profile cases, and Justice Kavanaugh was just settling into the Court. The 2019 term seemed likely to be different, in part because the Court's agenda included more high-profile cases, which could be expected to divide the Justices along ideological lines.

The Court's Decisions on the Merits

As it turned out, the Justices' voting patterns in cases with oral argument in the 2019 term resembled the preceding term in most respects. The Justices' proportions of liberal votes—again, in cases with clear ideological content—were arrayed as follows: Sotomayor 85%, Ginsburg 79%, Breyer 71%, Kagan 70%, Roberts 38%, Gorsuch 32%, Kavanaugh 30%, Alito 15%, and Thomas 12%. The gap in voting between the most liberal conservative (Roberts in 2019, Gorsuch in 2018) and the most conservative liberal (Kagan) was about the same as it had been in the preceding term. Conservative Justices divided into the same two subgroups as in 2018, but a little further apart from each other. The Court's liberals also split into the same two subgroups as in 2018.

---

characterized as conservative and liberal. (Thus, some cases treated as ideological in other sources are not included in the counts of votes in this chapter.) Cases that met this criterion were included if the Court reached decisions with opinions after hearing oral argument.

There were eight decisions with all conservatives on one side and all liberals on the other in the 2019 term, 15 percent of all cases with oral argument.[4] These included some of the major decisions of the term discussed in this volume. In one of those decisions, *Espinoza v. Montana Department of Revenue*, the Court held essentially that a state constitutional provision prohibiting government aid to religious schools violated the Free Exercise Clause of the First Amendment.[5] In another, *Seila Law v. Consumer Financial Protection Bureau*, the Court ruled that the limit on the president's power to remove the head of that bureau violated the constitutional separation of powers. In *Hernández v. Mesa*, the Court held that non-US citizens could not bring federal lawsuits based on a shooting by a government agent across an international border.[6]

But there were also six cases in which Roberts, Gorsuch, or Kavanaugh—or two of the three—voted with the Court's four liberals to create 5-4 or 6-3 majorities for liberal positions. Those defections explain why more than forty percent of the Court's decisions in cases with clear ideological content were decided in a liberal direction, despite the nominal 5-4 conservative advantage. Unlike the 2018 term, Roberts was distinctly more likely than Gorsuch or Kavanaugh to join his liberal colleagues: he took the liberal side in five of these six cases, compared with two each for Gorsuch and Kavanaugh. (Alito and Thomas, by contrast, sided with the liberal Justices in none of the major cases this year.) On the other side, there were five cases in which one or two of the liberal Justices joined the five conservative Justices in a conservative decision—Breyer most often, never Sotomayor.

The deviations from conservative positions taken by Roberts alone came in two of the most important decisions of the term, the Court's holding in *June Medical Services v. Russo* that a Louisiana regulation of abortion clinics was unconstitutional and its holding in *Department of Homeland Security v. Regents of the University of California* that the Trump administration had followed improper procedures when it eliminated the

---

[4]Justice Kagan was recused in one of these cases, so the vote was 5-3.
[5]See Chapter 5.
[6]See Chapters 6 and 13.

DACA program.[7] In *Bostock v. Clayton County*, Roberts and Gorsuch joined the Court's liberals in a 6-3 decision holding that employment discrimination based on sexual orientation or transgender status constitutes sex discrimination under Title VII of the Civil Rights Act of 1964.[8] And in *New York State Rifle & Pistol Association v. City of New York*, Roberts and Kavanaugh joined the liberals to create another 6-3 majority, this one to turn aside a challenge to a local gun regulation as moot because the regulation had been modified.[9]

Roberts' votes in the first three of those cases attracted considerable interest. Some observers of the Court have perceived a broader movement toward the ideological center by the Chief Justice during his first fifteen years in that role. From the perspective of some unhappy conservatives, Roberts has become the most recent example of a frequent pattern in which Justices appointed by Republican presidents establish moderate or even liberal records on the Court. Denounced by some conservatives after his votes created majorities for liberal rulings in a few important decisions in prior terms, Roberts received renewed criticism for his liberal positions in the 2019 term.[10]

Roberts' record in the 2019 term can be interpreted in different ways, but the extent of his liberalism should not be exaggerated. His overall voting record remained far more conservative than those of the relatively moderate liberals Breyer and Kagan. Still, it is intriguing that Roberts departed from the conservative fold in some major decisions. What accounts for these deviations? Roberts has expressed concern over perceptions of the Court as a partisan body, perceptions that reflect on his leadership as Chief Justice. Roberts may also be seeking to strengthen his reputation in another way by showing that he does not follow a consistent ideological line. And it is possible that he has reacted to changes in the political world over the past few years.

As in the 2018 term, Justices Gorsuch and Kavanaugh also had distinctly less conservative records than Justices Thomas and Alito. That

---

[7]See Chapter 7 on *June Medical* and Chapter 4 on *DHS v. University of California*.
[8]See Chapter 2.
[9]See chapter 11.
[10]Ronn Blitzer, "Roberts Drifts Away from Conservative Bloc, Angering Republicans and Exciting the Left," *Fox News* (1 July 2020).

difference is noteworthy because of the careful efforts of the Trump administration to select highly conservative Justices. Gorsuch is of particular interest, since his record over the last two terms is similar to that of Chief Justice Roberts. His liberal votes in some major 2019 cases may reflect both his strong commitment to textualism as a mode of legal interpretation and relatively liberal views about certain types of issues (such as Native Americans' rights).

Partisanship is a matter of interest in itself. Some cases, typically those that concern election issues or major presidential actions, have direct links to partisan conflict. In the 2019 term, the cases with the highest partisan stakes probably were the conflict over President Trump's effort to end the DACA immigration program, in which all the Justices except Roberts split along ideological lines, and the battles over subpoenas of Trump's financial records by a New York state prosecutor and by committees of the House of Representatives. Chief Justice Roberts wrote the Court's opinions in the two subpoena cases, securing 7-2 majorities for decisions that favored the president in some respects but not others. The dissenters, more favorable to Trump, were Justices Alito and Thomas.[11] That pair of decisions worked against perceptions of the Court as a partisan body, and Roberts' vote in the DACA case also supported an image that he stood above partisan considerations.

Preliminary Action: Staying Lower-Court Decisions

The Court's decisions in the cases it decides on the merits are certainly the most important part of its work. But the Court also decides whether to issue or vacate "stays" of actions by lower courts that prevent those actions from going into effect or continuing in effect. For example, if a Court of Appeals rules that a federal program is unconstitutional, a stay by the Supreme Court might allow the program to continue in operation while the Court considers the case. During the Trump administration, it has become more common for the federal government and its officials

---

[11]See chapter 14.

to seek stays by the Court of decisions by federal district courts before a court of appeals has ruled in a case. The Court has granted many of those stays. Although stays are a form of preliminary action in a case, some of the Court's stays have constituted its final word on a case.

From the beginning of the 2019 term through July 2020, the Court ruled on nine applications for stays of district court decisions by the federal government in decisions that evoked opinions or disagreements among the Justices. Five applications concerned criminal justice and four related to immigration, one of which also touched on environmental policy. The Court granted stays to the government or vacated the district court action in seven of the nine cases. In all but one case, either conservative or liberal Justices announced dissents from the Court's action.[12]

In three immigration-related cases and two criminal justice cases (involving execution of federal prisoners), the Court divided 5-4 along ideological lines in ruling for the government. The three immigration-related cases with 5-4 votes concerned denial of admission of noncitizens to the United States on the basis of their financial status (two cases) and the transfer of military funds to construct a wall on the border with Mexico. In one of the two cases in which the Court denied stays to the federal government, three of the conservative Justices announced their dissents; in the other, three conservatives would have modified the Court's ruling to make it more favorable to the government. Chief Justice Roberts was the only conservative who did not indicate disagreement with the majority in either case.

The Court also decided five cases involving stays of state election rules, three about absentee voting (in Wisconsin, Alabama, and Texas), one about the right of Floridians with felony convictions to vote, and one about Idaho's rules for signatures on petitions to put initiative measures on the ballot.[13] Leaving aside the Idaho case, the disputed election rules were thought to favor Republican electoral prospects. In two of those

---

[12]Justices who disagree with the Court's rulings on applications for stays do not always announce their dissents.

[13]The cases were *Republican National Committee v. Democratic National Committee* (Wisconsin); *Merrill v. People First of Alabama*; *Texas Democratic Party v. Abbott*; *Raysor v. DeSantis* (Florida) and *Little v. Reclaim Idaho*.

four cases, the Court stayed district court decisions that had invalidated those rules; in the other two, it upheld stays of district court invalidations by Courts of Appeals. Thus, all four decisions could be interpreted as favoring Republican interests. No Justices announced a dissent from the Texas decision, though Justice Sotomayor issued a brief opinion expressing her hope that the Court of Appeals would resolve the questions in the case well before the November election. All four liberal Justices dissented in the Wisconsin and Alabama cases; all but Breyer announced their dissents from the Florida decision.[14]

The Court's rulings on stay requests in the 2019 term provide additional evidence about the role of ideology in its work. The cases addressing the federal government's applications for stays involved issues on which conservatives and liberals often divide, so it may not be surprising that most of these cases evoked dissents from Justices in one ideological camp or the other. But historically, it had been highly unusual for the Court to grant stays of district court decisions prior to review by the Court of Appeals, and the willingness of the Court's conservative majority in the past few terms to grant government requests for these stays might be an indication of deference to the Trump administration that the liberal Justices do not share.[15] The 5-4 decisions in two of the absentee voting cases may reflect partisan considerations, in that all nine Justices took positions in these cases that were perceived to benefit their party. In the Florida case about voting by people with felony convictions, at least eight of the nine Justices did so. In that respect, these decisions look a little different from the 2019 decisions on the merits that involved the interests of the Republican and Democratic parties, especially the rulings on subpoenas of the president's financial records.

---

[14]In the Idaho case, Justices Sotomayor and Ginsburg dissented from a Court stay that prevented relaxation of the rules for gathering initiative signatures.
[15]See Stephen I. Vladeck, "The Solicitor General and the Shadow Docket," *Harvard Law Review* 133 (November 2019): 123–163.

Conclusions

It would be highly inaccurate to depict the current Supreme Court as a body in which liberal Democrats vote for liberal outcomes in each case and conservative Republicans vote for conservative outcomes. Many cases do not involve ideological issues. Even among the cases with ideological issues, decisions with all the conservatives on one side and all the liberals on the other side are the exception to the rule. Indeed, in the 2019 term it was about as common for the Court to rule unanimously in either a conservative or a liberal direction as it was to have a 5-4 vote with the conservative Justices on one side and the liberals on the other side. And even in nonunanimous decisions, it was common for conservative Justices to join with the liberal Justices to produce a liberal decision or for liberals to join with their conservative colleagues to increase the size of the majority for a conservative decision. In considerable part, those patterns stem from differences in the ideological positions of Justices who stand on the same side of the ideological spectrum. In the 2019 term, as in 2018, Justices Sotomayor and Ginsburg voted for liberal outcomes more often than the other two liberals. Similarly, Justices Thomas and Alito had more conservative records than their three conservative colleagues. For all these reasons, it is not surprising that there are a good many liberal decisions even on a Court with five conservative Justices.

Even so, there is a strong ideological element in decision-making on the current Supreme Court. The conservative Justices all vote for conservative outcomes much more often than any of the Court's liberals, while the liberal Justices take liberal positions far more often than any of the conservatives do. On cases that have the highest stakes for public policy or for the political parties, taken as a whole, the great majority of the Justices' votes fall on the side that we would expect based on their ideological leanings. The fact that the Court had five conservative Justices rather than five liberal members made considerable difference for its decisions. The appointment of Amy Coney Barrett as the sixth conservative will make a considerable difference as well. The Supreme Court's record in the 2019 term provides one more body of evidence that the outcomes of presidential elections have a fundamental effect on what the Court does.

Index